LET YOUR *Heart* OUT

HOW TO ESCAPE YOUR THOUGHTS AND RECONNECT WITH THE MOST IMPORTANT PART OF YOURSELF

STEFANI REINOLD, MD, MPH

Cover photo attributed to Authentic Portrait, LLC in Fairfax, VA

Publishing Services provided by Paper Raven Books
Printed in the United States of America
First Printing, 2018

Paperback ISBN= 978-0-9998391-0-2
Hardback ISBN= 978-0-9998391-1-9

Dedicated to my parents, Dan and Sheri,
For sacrificing so much so that I could follow my heart,
For modeling deep conversations,
For teaching me to look for the heart of the matter,
And above all, encouraging me to stay true to who I am.
I love you both.

TABLE OF CONTENTS

A Letter to the Reader

Thank you for picking up this book. Whether you were led here because you liked the title or the cover art, received this as a gift, or felt drawn to read this book by divine intervention, I am truly grateful that you are here. However you feel now, I believe that you are right where you are supposed to be. There are no accidents, no coincidences, and no regrets. Although you may not understand now, your life is a beautiful balance of pain and pleasure, trials and celebrations, mundane and milestones. You may want to clip out parts of your life, and you likely avoid many pain points. Remember this: you are you. Through the good and the bad, the thick and the thin, you are amazing.

My name is Stefani Reinold, and I'm a Board Certified psychiatrist, maternal mental health expert, wife, and mother. Some of you may know me from my rapidly growing online community, blog, and podcast. Others may know me from my online programs helping women overcome postpartum depression and anxiety. I've appeared on several podcasts and media outlets sharing my own personal struggles with postpartum depression. I also write and speak about eating disorders, body image, infertility, and loss.

I am extremely grateful for my platform as a psychiatrist, but I assure you that I never imagined becoming a *shrink*. I became a doctor to help people, and I became a psychiatrist because I loved hearing people's stories. While I dreamed of being a neurosurgeon who removed malignant brain tumors, I now take out tumors lodged in the most inconspicuous of places, unseen by our modern-day imaging capabilities and unheard of in our conscious awareness.

In my young career, I've witnessed the gamut of women's mental health issues. I've sat with the crying mother who just can't seem to bond with her new baby. I've seen the woman who couldn't leave her house after breaking up with her boyfriend. I've helped a woman after a violent suicide attempt almost two years after the birth of her baby. I've listened to the bizarre delusions of a mother of three who was certain that drones from above were poisoning her children's food. I've calmed a woman with debilitating obsessions and compulsions that impaired her ability to function in the world. I've comforted a woman who suffered yet another miscarriage and feared she may never be a mother. From bipolar, schizophrenia, and personality disorders to depression, anxiety, and trauma, I've seen it all. I've heard countless tales of women with addictions, eating disorders, and maladaptive coping.

I've helped women break through plateaus and rise up from rock bottom. I've empowered a mom in communicating her needs to her husband. I've taught a woman how to love her body again after birthing a baby. I've uncovered a mom's deep-seated limiting beliefs. I've investigated the hearts, souls, and minds of more than a thousand patients and have helped these women reconnect with what their heart most desires: their real selves.

Whether you are suffering from the most severe mental illness or just your run-of-the-mill life challenges, you're searching for authenticity. You're struggling to feel good enough in this world that constantly tells you that you are not enough. As women, we sacrifice bits of ourselves throughout our lives. How we reunite with those deepest intrinsic qualities of ourselves, or recreate a new identity altogether, is the crisis that we all face (some with more grace than others). Yet, the mystery of our identity remains. Who am I? What do I like and dislike? What do I want out of my life? We live our lives for something or someone else. We never stop to reflect: is this my true desire, or is someone else talking? Who is the real me?

After helping so many women uncover their real selves, I researched different ways to bring the same benefits of individual therapy to the masses. While I wish we could all afford individual therapy, we don't all have the funds or means. In the past five years, I have listened and reflected on not only what my patients and clients needed the most, but how I could help them uncover those truths on their own. I crafted a formula that I now share with you in this book, so you too can benefit from your own form of therapy.

May my own personal stories, and those of my patients (de-identified for confidentiality), present themselves as examples for reference, not as a source of comparison. My hope is that my transparency will serve as a foundation for trust and further work rather than resentment. In full transparency, it's important to mention that I am a woman of faith. It is only by the grace of God that I believe I have been able to get through challenging times in my life. Whether or not you are Christian, you need to find a strong foundation on which to build your life. Without a strong foundation, it is difficult to overcome the details of life. I hope my approach resonates on multiple levels, and I invite you to share this journey with me.

Think of this book as the prequel for future personal development work you do, like the *how to uncover your real desires* and *who you really are* to everyone else's *what to do* and *why you do it*. Before you can answer why, you first need to identify the who.

So, before you go prioritizing your life or writing your obituary or designing your perfect day, read this book.

To my beloved patients, I'm forever grateful for the opportunity to be your doctor, your psychiatrist, your soul healer. To my reader, I sincerely appreciate the opportunity to let my heart out to you. Because this process was so healing for me, I invite you to connect with me and other readers. If you would like to continue the conversation and let your heart out, please visit www.letyourheartout.com. I look forward to connecting with you.

From the bottom of my heart,

Stefani

PART 1

The Heart

Who am I, I dare not say
For if I do, I cannot say
What will I be, no one will know
How can I tell, my heart does hold
The secrets of me, the truth of me
The best of me, in one piece
Bound by strings
Who am I, I dare not say

-Stefani Reinold

1
Losing Heart

Who am I? I thought to myself. I was sitting on the couch in my maternity pants and tank top, messy bun atop my head. It was 11 am on a Saturday, and gazing out the window, I saw the most beautiful clear sky and soft breeze blowing through the trees. It looked so enticing. Why couldn't I muster the energy to bring myself out of this state? To walk outside and enjoy the wonder of this crisp winter day? My nine-month-old Kate loved to go outside. A walk always kept her calm, the rhythmic bobs of the stroller lulling her to sleep. She didn't need to be calmed though. She was a great baby and already a great sleeper.

I should take advantage of this quality time, I thought. *Today is my only day off this week, and with my mom in town, we have the perfect opportunity. We could drive into the city to walk around the National Mall and soak in the sacred history of our nation's capital.* (We'd been in Washington, D.C. for a year and had yet to explore the city.) But I couldn't. I was stuck, out of touch with the most wondrous parts of me, paralyzed by the darkness that had overcome me.

"You don't look so good," my mom commented, interrupting me from my thoughts. She was making her way from the kitchen into the living room. With her coffee in hand, she sat down on the loveseat by the adjacent wall. Clearly, she was taken aback by my lack of hygiene that had become the norm alongside this loss of enthusiasm about life. While our appearance is not always the best indicator of our internal pain, it certainly was for me at this time, as my struggle to take care of myself matched my struggling underneath. I didn't know it at the time, but I was suffering from postpartum depression.

"Well, I don't feel so good... but thanks, mom." I offered a forced smile, continuing to face the window. Watching the solitude of nature put me in a trance. It had been nine months since Kate was born, but I still felt like I was walking through sludge. For the typically bubbly morning person that I am, this was not me.

"I'm just worried about you, honey. I mean, have you even eaten breakfast?" asked my mom, the ultimate caretaker, always putting others before herself.

I don't know. Have I eaten breakfast?

"Can I make you something?" I guess she took it as a sign when I didn't respond.

"Uh, sure, I guess," I mumbled.

"Well, what would you like?" my mom offered.

Really, I have to make a decision right now? What do I want for breakfast? It's a simple choice. Why is it so hard for me to make a decision? Maybe my mom will just make something, and then I'll eat it.

"All right, how about just some eggs?" Thank goodness she took the bait and made the decision for me. Trying to make a decision was just not happening.

"Yeah, that's fine," I quickly replied.

"Do you want them scrambled or what?"

How did I like my eggs? I don't know anymore. Do I even like eggs?

"Sure, scrambled is fine." I shrugged. I finally turned my head away from the window. My eyes met my mom's gaze. I couldn't communicate consciously, but I was screaming for help unconsciously. My mom could tell. She knew the "I'm fines" had reached their expiration date. This was more than a bad day or self-induced misery. This was something different.

I searched her face for answers. Clarity. Comfort. Calm. She just looked at me. Her face spoke volumes. I'd never seen my mom look so... concerned. I could see she was trying to hold back tears. *Wow, I must look worse than I thought.*

"Are you going to be okay?" my mom probed. She was returning to Texas the next day. Travis was deployed on a short-term training assignment for the Army. I would be alone with Kate for the next six weeks.

"Yeah, I guess so..." I paused. My mind was racing with thoughts and worries. I wasn't sure I could tell her the truth.

"I mean, I'm not even sure what my work benefits are. I could call my job and see if I could take a medical leave. I could stay here and help you out while Travis is away," she suggested. I could tell she was feeling the same powerlessness that I felt inside. I had made her feel this way. I had projected these feelings of inadequacy onto her.

I was silent. I wanted her to stay. I really did. How could I admit that to her? What if she lost her job over me? I've always been so independent. I didn't need someone to take care of me. How could I reassure her when I couldn't even reassure myself?

"Stefani, you know I'd do anything for you." Her words were more rushed, less deliberate, like she'd been holding her breath and was finally able to release the biggest sigh. "I want to take care of you. I *have* to take care of you. I have to know you're safe. You have to be okay." Her last words felt more like a command than reassurance.

Stefani, you know you're not okay, my heart spoke up. *Just tell her you're not okay. Tell her to stay.* But *I am okay*, I kept telling myself. I needed to tell her. She needed to know. She needed to know that I'd be okay.

"I made an appointment with a psychiatrist this week." There. I said it. I finally admitted it to someone. Yes, the psychiatrist is seeing a psychiatrist. Although I am a mental health professional myself, making that appointment was possibly one of the most difficult decisions of my life. I did not grow up in a family keen on mental health care and had several biases and judgments toward the profession before deciding to pursue it. The fact that I became a psychiatrist still strikes me as comical.

"Okay, when is it?" my mom implored.

Wait, no judgment? No opinion? Huh, didn't expect this kind of reaction. It's so... matter-of-fact. I should've opened up to her months ago. "Tomorrow, actually. Can you watch Kate in the morning? Then I can take you to the airport tomorrow afternoon." My mind was still reeling that she was being so patient, so calm. I guess I'm not sure what I really expected, but given my parents' reactions toward mental health professionals growing up, I certainly did not expect such neutrality.

"Of course! I'd love to." She smiled. This smile was more than the joy of a grandmother spending time with her only granddaughter though. This smile was the peace of a mother knowing that her daughter will be okay.

Most of that time in my life, I have laid to bed, but I'll never forget how slowed down I felt. I was drowning inside, barely hanging on. My heart was dying a slow death. My brain was functioning on low power mode. For a year, my whole life felt out of control and chaotic; what's worse is that I actually didn't care. I had stopped showering daily, wore my hair in the messy mom bun more days than not, and overall felt completely detached, not only from my daughter but from my life. This was not me. Although I knew this was *not* me, I didn't know what *was* me, and I had no way of knowing who I was. I had filled my life with goals, accomplishments, activities, and behaviors. I lost touch with the heart of the issue.

Just be you, they say. Do what's right for you, they say. You be you, let me be me, they say. What does it all mean? How can I be me if I don't even know who that person is? Is it even possible to characterize myself in earthly terms? How can I get to the bottom of my heart? My mind was swimming in a labyrinth of questions. As I answered one, I opened new doors to ten more unanswered questions. The more doors of my heart I opened, the more perplexed I became. I knew there had to be an easier way to just be me. As I coursed through the maze of my mind, a vivid childhood memory came to consciousness.

"Why did you kick her in the shins?!" my dad yelled in disbelief after the referee gave me a red card in soccer and sentenced me to the sidelines.

"Because she took the ball from me," lamented my five-year-old self.

"Well, that's part of soccer. To take the ball and run it down the field and score goals." I'm sure my dad explained the game better than this. He's a great coach, but I don't have the best memory when it comes to my five-year-old self.

"Well, she's bigger than me," I whined.

My dad paused for a moment before a big smile slowly curled up the sides of his lips, and he looked me directly in the eyes. "Stefani, a lot of the girls may be bigger than you, but always remember, you have heart." And he was right. I did have heart.

I've heard this story many times. It's become the running story in my household that I'm the only five-year-old ever to get a red card in youth soccer. You better believe that my storyteller dad will share this story with anyone who will listen. I used to take attacks on my feistiness as an insult, but given that I played in a six-year-old league when I was five and most of the girls were a head taller than me, I'm impressed I could hold my own. But why was I remembering this story now? What did heart have to do with my postpartum depression?

My dad used the word heart a lot when my brothers and me were growing up. I heard the words "heart" and "character" more than any other words. I never really knew what he meant. I assumed on different occasions it meant different things: work ethic, drive, integrity, moxie, achievement. But I did realize that heart wasn't something to be chased. It was something deep inside us, pumping the blood of life into our being, similar to our biological heart.

I remember the first time I watched a real heart beating. As a sophomore pre-medicine student at Baylor University, I shadowed a cardiothoracic surgeon performing coronary artery bypass surgery. Coronary artery bypass surgery is quite miraculous if you think about it. We have the technology to put someone to sleep, control their pain, stop their heartbeat, put them on artificial life support as we repair their heart, restart their heart at the end of the procedure, and wake them up. Watching the surgeons work with such ease and precision was remarkable. I was in awe. I observed the detail with which they sewed together new arteries—often taken from the leg—to the coronary arteries of the heart, all while the patient was being sustained by artificial life support.

The most miraculous part of the procedure is near the end. The patient is slowly taken off of bypass, and the surgeon resuscitates the heart through electroshock or manual massage, bringing life back into the patient. Reflecting on this experience, I concluded that I was living on life support. I was sustained by the details of life, but I lost the core of what mattered most. I was in desperate need of a revival. Fortunately, the heart of our mind is amazingly adaptable. Much like the biological heart, the heart of our mind can be strengthened or weakened through work of the individual.

Outside of the medical world, the word "heart" has gotten a bad rap. We have diminished heart to pithy catch phrases and quote boards, and sayings like "follow your heart" and "whatever your heart desires" portray the heart as either some woo-woo, ethereal entity out of grasp from us mere mortals or some lusty greed fueled by a power trip. The heart is neither of these things. It is not reserved for use by the most mindful and centered beings. And it is not some evil, wrong, or bad part of ourselves.

Even so, heart evokes feelings more than possibly any other word in the dictionary. Think about the words heartwarming, heartfelt, or heartbroken, or idioms like "you touched my heart" or "you broke my heart." You can't escape feeling something when you hear these words. While the heart can be the impetus for feelings and behaviors, heart is not an action or an emotion. Heart is deeper, more intrinsic to you. You can *have* heart and you can *lose* heart. You can also uncover your heart, though you cannot gain heart.

Simply put, *your heart is the most important, essential part of yourself.*

Some people call it your authentic self, your spirit, your inner child, or your true self. I call it your heart. It is the consummation of the best, most beautiful parts of yourself, all wrapped up into one entity. I say part, not parts, because this is one solid core of you, not dismembered multiples. Like the biological heart, you cannot see the heart in your mind without radical surgical intervention. You know your heart only by the feeling that it emits. You feel the rhythm of its beat. When you are seeking your heart, what you are truly seeking is a feeling of truth, of being one with the *you* that you want to be, living beyond the fluff of the world and finding the deepest, truest part of you.

Your heart is one being that flows freely through life, living out its purpose without the blemishes and imperfections of the world clouding its beauty. Children are perhaps the best example of heart-centered living. When I remember that little girl on the soccer field, I remember a little girl full of heart, full of feeling. I remember it again in my gymnastics meets as a child, performing in oratorical speaking contests, writing poems, or playing dress-up.

What happened to us? We used to be the fun-loving, creative, spunky, fiery little girls with more dreams than we could ever fulfill in a lifetime. Just talk to any six-year-old girl and you hear joy, hope, and excitement. My daughter changes her mind by the second. One day, she wants to be a YouTube sensation (wow, how the dreams are a-changin'). Next day, she wants to be a doctor. Other days, she dreams of being a real-life princess or a nurse or a teacher. Some days, she talks about being a mommy just like me (*swoon...*). Little girls live in pure bliss. They're not worried about their dress size, what their body looks like, what so-and-so thinks of them, or how they will get through the day. They just are.

We also can think of those amazingly talented athletes who had great abilities, but often never achieved greatness in their chosen sport because they lacked heart. You can feel it in their presence. You can see it on their faces. And, usually, these are the same people who will likely end up turning to drugs or other addictions in order to *feel* something. News flash! We have all become like those talented individuals with no heart. I look around me now and see a mass crisis of individuals who have lost heart. Not only have we lost heart in the inner-drive sense of the word, but we've lost it in the entirety of our lives. Ask anyone around you what their current mood is and you're bound to hear one of the following: tired, stressed, busy, overwhelmed, exhausted. Some of the more honest ones will admit, "I don't know."

We have now become accustomed to running through life on low power mode or, worse, completely empty. We don't even know the difference between living from the heart and running on fumes. We have accepted the mantra: life is hard, suck it up. And we are pretty good at sucking it up. We play by the rules, put on a pretty face, and do the right things, all the while slowly losing ourselves.

I could go on a rant about societal and cultural pressures on women and that all of this synthesizes down to a feminist issue. I'll spare y'all the lecture. I must admit, though, that feminism is not the answer. It's not about equality or changing work requirements or making others cater to women. I know there's more to the feminism argument (don't send me hate mail), but this book is not about feminism. If that's your jam, I won't stop you. Feminism is not the issue here though. This is a matter of the heart, and matters of the heart cannot be solved with regulation or systems or even different cultural standards. Matters of the heart start and end with the heart.

A long-term patient of mine, Jenna, remarked in a therapy session, "I feel like I've lost myself." She paused and then replied, "I mean, who *am* I?" probing me as if I could offer her solace in her despair. I wish I could say that Jenna was alone, but the more women I connect with, the more I hear the same recount over and over again. *Who am I?* has become our mantra. We throw the question out into the universe hoping for a reply. When we put our faith in the world, we continue to lose ourselves to the world bit-by-bit.

You don't have to suffer from postpartum depression to lose your heart. Although rock bottom moments can shake us up more than others, I worry more about the subtle drifters. I drifted subtly for years before the onset of my postpartum depression. I experienced minor rock bottom moments prior to my depression as well. Judgment from elementary school bullies. Inadequacy of adolescent angst. Conflict with my parents. Pressures of undergraduate pre-medicine classes. Unworthiness of my body. Heartbreak from failed romantic relationships. Loneliness from lack of social support. Being overwhelmed by medical school classes. Despair from enduring an Army deployment.

After each battle we face, pieces of our heart become casualties to the cause. When we experience judgment, we start to change ourselves to avoid future whiplash. When we face conflict, we concede our passions for the sake of the relationship. When we undergo pressure, we mount up defenses to strengthen us for future stress. When we suffer heartbreak, we submit to others' desires to avoid pain of abandonment. When we face loneliness, we surrender our uniqueness to fit in with social norms and standards. Until, one day, we wake up and can no longer recognize ourselves. We no longer see *who we are*, but rather, we are plagued by *what we have*.

On the surface, I had it all: loving husband, supportive family, gracious God, beautiful half a million-dollar home with a magnificent tree-lined view outside Washington, D.C., and a healthy baby girl. I was living my childhood dream as a doctor. I was physically fit. And I was miserable. Inside, I felt as though nothing added up. All the dreams of my childhood had actually come true, yet, I had never felt so empty. While I had achieved external success, I had lost my internal sense of self along the way. I questioned my interests, doubted my passions, and suppressed my fears. All the while, I was ashamed of the frustration that I felt.

Frustration arises from the desire to escape. We feel trapped. Our heart is trapped inside a box that others outside of ourselves have designed. We have added a lot of fancy wrapping paper and glitter and bows to decorate the box, but we still haven't opened the gift box. Hence, we don't ever actually *feel* different when all of the things around us change. We can change all the details of our lives, but if the change is happening on false premises of who we are, we will continue to suffer. As my pastor says, perfect environment will never solve the problem because perfect environment is not the problem. The problem is a suffocation of our heart. Until we let our heart out, we will continue to flow through the mundane of life. We will fight the ever-rising sensation of inadequacy and defend our value in the world through superficial means.

In the past five years, I have treated thousands of patients. I have counseled more than a handful of friends. I have listened to hundreds of women. I have heard a myriad of chief complaints including trouble sleeping, lack of energy, poor focus, difficulty communicating with the husband, strained friendships, or trouble at work. I have also observed clinical manifestations of anxiety, worry, stress, depression, and trauma. I have seen the daily challenges in balancing work and family, finding good childcare, making self-care a priority, and carving out time for daily personal hygiene.

I often prescribe medications, recommend treatments, give encouragement, or provide strategies to overcome these supposed problems. The problem is not the lack of solutions. The problem is not identifying the core of the problem in the first place, which lies far beneath the level of conscious awareness. The problem is a crisis of identity and the ensuing lack of clarity. Without being clear on who and what you are, no amount of knowledge, information, or solutions will ever solve the essence of the problem. No matter the ailment, no solution will solve the problem unless you first solve the mystery of you.

Being you requires a state of being, an unwavering acceptance of what is, a radical processing of what was, and a sincere excitement of what will be. Being is not doing. Being is living from the heart. This is where the barrier lies. We have lost the most important, essential part of ourselves. With that, we have lost our foothold. We have forgotten how to feel, how to be. We have lost our hearts.

2
What Women Want

What Women Want. It's not only the title of Mel Gibson's one-hit-wonder of a chick flick but also describes dating books and coaching workshops. It's the butt of countless sitcom jokes. It's become humorous for us to laugh at the fact that women are complicated and emotional and crazy (although I prefer the term mysterious). No one ever actually talks about what women want, though. We just bounce around the topic and then men around the world throw up their hands in frustration.

"Stefani, what do you want?" my mom asked comforting me.

"I don't know!" I cried through sobs of tears.

I was vacationing at the lake in Horseshoe Bay outside Austin, Texas for the 4th of July. Yet, instead of relaxing, I was meticulously calculating what my GPA would be dependent on theoretical grades I would make this coming academic year. I had finished out my sophomore year of college with a few Bs and Cs, and in the pre-medicine world, this is a death sentence. I had been a nervous wreck since the spring semester concluded. It also didn't help that my boy crush du jour had stopped calling and texting me, spiraling me into a downward doom.

"Do you want to be a doctor?" my mom whispered gently. My parents always wanted what was best for me. The road to becoming a doctor is a hard, long road. It is not for the faint of heart. From early in my studies, I doubted the path, as is common with any daunting delayed-gratification venture. My vacillation became a source of constant angst between me and my parents.

"I don't know!" It was true. In that moment, I felt so confused and hopeless.

"Well, you know, we just want you to be happy," my mom encouraged.

"What if I don't know what I want to do?" I think every college kid faces the age-old identity crisis when pondering the "what do you want to do" question. I was no exception.

"Why don't you write a bucket list?" my dad suggested.

My dad has always had a knack for coming up with the best ideas. In that hotel room at the lake, I pulled out hotel paper and pen, and instead of calculating my hypothetical future GPA, I wrote my bucket list. Sadly, I no longer have that sheet of paper, which probably got thrown out during my minimalism crusade last year or maybe is still at my parents' house, who knows. I do know that I shared my heart and soul on that piece of paper all those years ago. It was the first time I can remember deliberately and consciously attempting to answer the question, what do I want?

Apparently, I wanted about 200+ things. Of course, I don't remember all of the items on my bucket list, but a few still stick out in my mind: graduate medical school, get married, do something important, own horses, have a ranch in Texas, have babies, go skydiving, run a marathon, travel the world, own my own business, publish a book. My list was not that surprising.

Yet, every item on the list did not matter by itself. It was the feeling attached to it that excited me.

I thought, *When I graduate medical school, I will feel important. When I get married, I will feel complete. When I do something important, I will feel worthy. When I own horses, well, I don't know what I'll feel (since I hadn't ridden a horse since my pony party at seven years old). When I have a ranch in Texas, I will feel peaceful. When I have babies, I will feel full. When I go skydiving, I will feel free. When I travel the world, I will feel adventurous. When I run a marathon, I will feel healthy. When I own my own business, I will feel in control. When I publish a book, I will feel accomplished.*

What did I really want? What is it that all women want? Well, I'm about to tell you what women want. Get ready. Grab a pen and a piece of paper. This will be revolutionary. What do women want?

They want chocolate and attention. *JK!* That's just what my husband thinks. (Though, he's not that far off.)

What do women really want?

They want to *feel whole*.

And how does that happen? By living from the heart.

Think about it. Every single womanly desire that you ever hear has to do with that one thing: living a fuller life, free from baggage, from the deepest part of their authentic self, their heart. Sure, they want the husband, babies, a nice home, cute decorations. They want ladies' nights, diamonds, presents, love notes, bubble baths, and romance. They want daily pleasures that may bring a reprieve from the utility of life.

On a daily basis, though, women don't want all of these things. If you received flowers every day, it would no longer be special. And if you ate chocolate at every meal, you may get sick of it (maybe). What you really want on a daily basis is not an entity outside of yourself. It's the yearning and longing from deep within you, the heartbeat waiting to be heard. You're longing to live from your heart, from the inside out, not outside in.

While I am extremely proud of accomplishing my childhood dreams, my accomplishments don't give me a warm hug at night. We aren't chasing dreams in a vacuum. We're chasing dreams because of the way we perceive they will make us feel. And that is where good marketing comes in play. If someone can convince you that you will feel differently after buying a product, going through a course, or consuming an item, then that is money. (You can thank me later for the best marketing advice ever.)

We have let the noise around us cloud what we really want. We have completely lost touch with the true desires of our heart. We now fleet from one self-improvement strategy to the next. What we really want to change is not a matter outside of ourselves. What we really want is to live from the *heart*, a life led by *feeling* the constant, steady beat of our heart.

Even in the throes of my postpartum depression, all that I really wanted was to feel whole again. I felt broken off and disjointed, giving of myself to the myriad of forces around me: my job, my baby, my husband, my family. All the while, I was disconnecting further from the desires of my heart.

Disconnected from our Heart's Desires

Whether or not you suffer from postpartum depression or some other mental illness, you are inundated by the same prevailing message from society: you are not good enough. When we hear this message millions of times a day, it is easy to conform our actions and behaviors to meet the demands of society.

> Not thin enough? I'll work to lose weight.
> Not pretty enough? I'll wear makeup.
> Not stylish enough? I'll buy more stylish clothes.
> Not confident enough? I'll learn to speak up.
> Not quiet enough? I'll learn to shut up.
> Not rich enough? I'll get a side hustle.

We assume that by changing our actions, we will drown out the pain. All we really crave is a different feeling, which can only be felt from the beating of our heart, not from the superficial ties that bind us. Therefore, the majority of the actions we take in our lives, are an effort to mask this underlying belief that we are not enough just as we are. No matter how hard we try, we never reach the state of enough-ness that we crave.

Because nothing we *do* will ever change how we *feel*. In fact, the *more* we do, the *less* we feel. What happens over time is self-destruction, self-sabotage, and self-mutilation. Literally. Whether through body hatred, substance abuse, or mental illness, loss of heart is expressed in brokenness. We can also appreciate a loss of heart when we tie our self-worth to the fleeting tethers of this world, like our physical bodies, love, or money.

We try to mold our bodies to fit the culturally acceptable "ideal body." About 90% of women are dissatisfied with their bodies, and more than 75% of women endorse disordered eating.[1] True story. We've been brainwashed to believe that the only way to be happy and healthy is to have perky boobs, no cellulite, and chiseled abs. We don't want to be thinner just to be thinner. Sure, maybe our clothes would fit better, but really, that's not the biggest reason. The before and after weight loss testimonials say it all: my life was horrible, I was depressed, lonely, and fat, and now I feel better than ever, I met my spouse, and I'm happy, healthy, and fit. We're chasing that *feeling*. It's not about the body. The problem begins early in childhood. According to the National Eating Disorders Association, 42 percent of first-to third-grade girls want to lose weight, and 81 percent of 10-year-olds are afraid of being fat. According to a study in the medical journal *Pediatrics*, about two-thirds of girls in the 5th to 12th grades said that magazine images influence their vision of an ideal body, and about half of the girls said the images made them want to lose weight.[2]

By adolescence, studies show that young people are receiving an estimated 5,260 "attractiveness messages" per year from network television commercials alone. According to *Teen* magazine, 35 percent of girls ages 6 to 12 have been on at least one diet, and 50 to 70 percent of normal weight girls think they are overweight.[2] Boys are not excluded. Body dissatisfaction and subclinical eating disordered behaviors—including binge eating, purging, laxative abuse, and fasting for weight loss—are nearly as common among males as they are among females.[3]

While these articles and research studies portray the state of youth in the United States, I know from personal and professional relationships with non-Americans, the struggle is ubiquitous. Likely due to the influence of the Internet and social media, American problems tend to leak to other countries.

Our obsession with the ideal body evolves into body hatred in some cases. We literally begin to mutilate our bodies through cutting and self-injurious behaviors, which are on the rise. Nearly 13% of ninth graders engaged in some form of cutting or self-injurious behaviors in the past month.[4] But this isn't about the food or our bodies. This is about the feeling that we are trying to create for ourselves. We will do anything to feel something, if even physically.

If we are not trying to feel something by changing our bodies, we try to feel something by seeking love. We have been conditioned to believe that once we find "the One," we will be happy and everything in the world will be good. By our mid-twenties, many of us define our personal sense of self-worth by whether or not we are married, or by how much money we make. A huge misconception given to young girls, especially, is that a man will "complete" you (thank you, *Jerry Maguire*). While I am a happily married woman and my life has been abundantly better since marrying my husband, I am the first to admit that my husband did not solve all my problems. If anything, he made my life more complicated (I still love you, honey!). As they say, marriage is a problem-creating device, not a problem-solving device. I agree. A husband will not fulfill that aching void in your soul like you're hoping for.

Now, beyond our bodies and love, the next crutch we entangle our hearts with is money. With financial stressors being the number one cause of divorce and psychological distress, I'd venture to guess that the majority of us have our own entanglements with money. Let's also consider the thousands of side hustles being formed each and every day. One can easily conclude that job satisfaction is generally low, particularly in the millennial generation. Chances are, you came across the same online marketing gurus that I did, the ones who show a beautiful picture of a perfect body, perfect marriage, best kids, the multi-million-dollar home complete with smiles, tears, and the feeling of true happiness. It's not really about more money. We want the *feeling* that comes with more money.

We have also betrayed our childhood passions and interests. Few adults know what it means to play. And even if they do, they do not make time for play. We instead live out our playful fantasies vicariously through our own children. Satisfaction and contentment in work, play, and love was once considered to be the trifecta of psychological health. We have fractured ourselves, thus affecting our ability to enjoy work, play, or love. In order to reconnect to the lost parts of ourselves, we must first look past the pleasantries and get to the core of the problem. If we are going to let our heart out, we must find the heart in the first place, because what you're doing now is probably causing more harm than good.

3
Why Self-Help Is Hurting the Self

"Ugh, I can't do it anymore," I argued with myself as I crumpled up yet another piece of paper and threw it in the trash.

"Uh... can't do what?" my husband mocked at my pathetic display.

"It's different every time." Still frustrated with myself.

"What's different?" My clearly confused husband questioned.

"My scores," I grumbled.

"Okkkaaayyyy..." as he gave me the face that communicates, you're so crazy, but I love you anyway. (Unfortunately, this was not the first time he has given me that face, and I guarantee it won't be the last.) He was perplexed. I don't blame him. I had recently developed a habit of escaping off with my laptop to work on "my business" or, rather, doing another online course or reading another self-help book or personal development series.

After overcoming postpartum depression, I continued to feel emptiness inside. My first step into recovery was not the journey to my heart; it was a venture into more and more of the same. We often repeat patterns of coping and mechanisms of change, hence the power of my unconscious coping mechanisms at play. It would take me a couple of years to begin to uncover the deeper issues. In the meantime, I cloaked the issues in more stuff. I traded one sense of accomplishment for another. Except, this time, my achievement status did not stem in diplomas or material goods; it branched from the excellence of self-improvement.

I was going through a popular online biz personal development course and kept getting hung up on my initial priority scores. The lesson asks you to rank different areas of your life from one to ten. This is the most important step, because the rest of the course hinges on finding your lowest scores and improving on them. Yet, every time I went through it, I gave myself different rankings. Some days, I even felt so great that most of the categories of my life were given scores of eight or nine. Other days, it seemed as though all of my scores were in the three to four range. Maybe I *was* crazy. I have since gone through several self-development courses and faced similar feelings of vacillation and indecision.

I didn't use to be indecisive. You can ask my mom. In fact, I was so decisive that I knew exactly how I wanted my hair to look and would proceed to have my mom redo it at least three times in the mornings. And, still, I'd be in tears because my hair would not look exactly as I had wanted it. As a little girl, I was decisive about many things beyond my hair. By the age of 10, I wanted to be a doctor (or the President of the United States, it was a toss-up), get married, have a big family, have a golden retriever, travel the world, live on the East Coast, publish a book, and be a motivational speaker. And I had the rather unique goal of "doing something that no other woman has done." This goal came after an oratorical speech where I researched amazing women, like Amelia Earhart and Margaret Thatcher. I wanted to be like them, to be able to impact history in a way that the lives of women changed forever. Well, in no particular order, I got all of those things (err almost—still working on the changing the world bit).

Through it all, I noticed that dreaming is a lot more fun than accomplishing. When you dream, you can avoid thoughts, feelings, or beliefs that cause you pain. After you accomplish something, nothing changes. Dreaming is doing while accomplishing is just being. Doing is a cheap scapegoat.

Despite having a deeply-rooted sense of self as a little girl, I lost myself along the way. I began to question my dreams and my goals. Had it not been for my supportive parents and the grace of God, I never would have made it through medical school. I've now come to accept that no one makes it out of childhood unscathed. I have some of the best parents a girl could ask for, yet I faced my share of heartache and trials, some self-inflicted and some stemming from external pressures. Somewhere along the way, I began drifting from my heart.

When we lose touch with our heart, we lose all decision-making capability. In fact, indecisiveness can be one of the biggest tells for a woman straying from a heart-centered life. Think of the number of times you say the words, "I don't know" in a given day. I would venture to guess that you *do* know, but after years of suppressing your deepest desires, wants, and needs, you do not feel worthy of sharing what you know. And when we don't make decisions for ourselves, others will make them for us.

I began living for boys, for my parents, for friends, for accomplishments, for goals, and for others. I felt shame for the parts of myself that didn't fit into the molds of others. And I came to believe I was damaged goods, that because I could not make these systems fit into my life, I was not only failing, but I was a failure. In my world, there was nothing worse.

The pressure to conform to external influences is real. These days, it's not enough to have the ideal body, fulfilling career, great husband, 2.5 children (what does that even mean anyway?), golden retriever, and beautiful million-dollar home in the suburbs. Now, you need to have the side hustle and social media platform and speaking gigs on top of the lucrative full-time job. The mounting expectations on women is nothing sheer of lunacy.

Over time, we realize that none of these things will bring the feelings that we are hoping for. By then, we have likely fallen prey to the trance of self-development. Traditional self-development is alluring and seductive. It does very little in actually uncovering the self though. Let me share a story with you to explain what I mean.

I played golf in high school. I remember in one particular tournament, I hit my ball into every single water hazard on the course. Every. Single. One. Needless to say, this was not the highlight of my golf career. The most frustrating part was a conversation I had with a fellow golf friend of mine after the tournament.

"Stefani, how'd you do?" Leslie asked, chipper as ever. She was already projected to win the tournament even before her fabulous score hit the scoreboard.

"Ehh… I don't want to talk about it," I glared down at my scorecard, hoping that she would leave me alone. Now.

"Was it the water?"

Yes. "Nah," I shrugged it off. "I don't know. I just wasn't in it today." This was partially true. My mental blocks clearly had something to do with me hitting my ball into every single water hazard. That's sports psychology 101 for you.

"You know, I hated this course the first time I played. I hit every single water hazard. I was so pissed with myself."

Wait, did I hear her right? Did she just admit that she played as poorly as I did the first time through this course? Maybe there's hope for me yet. After this enlightening moment, I was irked. Why had no one mentioned to me all the water hazards on this course? Maybe it wouldn't have made a difference, but maybe it would have.

Well, this may not be a golf game, but I still owe it to you to point out the biggest hazard that you face on this journey. The biggest hazard standing in your way is the allure of traditional self-development.

These days, it seems we are all searching for our most authentic self. Different experts have different words for it: your priority, your intention, your joy, your life satisfaction, your greatness. Others describe it more as an action: what gets you excited, what lights you up, what makes you come alive. Or some people talk about it in terms of your time: what could you spend your whole day doing, how would you spend your perfect day, what would you do on vacation. Or your legacy: what do you want to be remembered for, what do you want your kids to say about you.

If you can package a method helping people dream about a fantastical dream future, you've got yourself a gold mine. In fact, Americans spend $11 billion annually on "self-help" books.[5] That doesn't even include the multi-millions that are spent on online courses, webinars, workshops, seminars, and live events. The number of multi-millionaires is endless. Some of the wealthiest people in the world, like Tony Robbins, Deepak Chopra, and Oprah, fall into the self-development space.

Yet, the self-help industry has become like the diet industry in that it feeds on itself. It is becoming more well-accepted that diets do not work.[6] Recent evidence reveals that diets actually lead to long-term weight *gain*, not weight loss. Still, the diet industry prevails. The industry instills a theoretical problem and makes false promises to solve this problem. Knowing that diets do not work and that it is only a matter of time before an individual will seek yet another diet, the industry continues to feed itself. The diet industry prevails, not *despite* its cockeyed claims, but *because* of its cockeyed claims. If diets led to health and permanent weight loss, the industry would cease to exist.

Similarly, the self-help industry is flooded with shams and proselytizers who claim if you only follow X, Y, and Z, then you will have a happy, healthy, and perfect life. If these stepwise approaches worked, we wouldn't continue to experience inadequacy and self-misery. Just as diets lead to worse health outcomes, traditional self-help resources exacerbate the problems of the self, because traditional self-help does nothing to actually connect with the heart. What if I told you that self-development as we know it speaks to only 5% of who we are? True story. Research shows that our unconscious mind runs 95% of our daily activity.[7] That means the majority of our decisions, actions, emotions, and behaviors depend on the 95% of brain activity that is beyond our conscious awareness. As such, a large part of our heart remains unconscious.*

Not only that, but our unconscious mind operates much faster and more efficiently than our conscious mind. Our unconscious mind operates at 40 million bits of data per second, whereas the conscious mind processes at only 40 bits per second.[8] In essence, our unconscious is much more powerful than the conscious mind. Therefore, our lives are largely run by our unconscious mind.

The proficiency of our unconscious state works in our favor. Our brain has the brilliant ability to create patterns and imprints of mundane life events, so we do not waste unnecessary energy accomplishing each and every chore of our daily life. We also don't need to expend significant mental energy to orchestrate the wondrous symphony of millions of physiological processes that occur every second of every day. Breathing. Digestion. Balance. Sleep. These are all miraculous examples of the complex

---

* Unconscious and subconscious seem synonymous in pop culture. Different therapy styles use different words to mean the same thing. For purposes of this book, I use the word unconscious.

interplay of thousands of biological systems that are under the control of our unconscious.

Beyond our bodily processes, our unconscious mind is the biggest determinant of our personality, and thus, our heart. Our unconscious is the one frame of reference that we can use to best answer the question, who am I? And until you uncover the unconscious, you will never truly be able to be you or embrace the most essential part of you: your heart. The problem with some 12-week self-help courses is that no matter how much you control your conscious mind, you will continue to flounder in the 95% of unconscious waters of your life. You cannot begin to cure the complex issues of the unconscious mind by changing the 5% of your conscious state of awareness.

When we begin to run our entire lives on autopilot, we easily start to lose ourselves. Over time, we have become a mass of unconscious habits rather than conscious intentions. We then face a true identity crisis. Our unconscious has been leading our life, based on false premises of who we are, mind you. We no longer know who we are, what we want, or how we want to live.

Simply put, your unconscious is *you*. Therefore, to be you requires reconnection with the unknown parts of yourself. Meaning, we need to uncover your unconscious, because it's your unconscious that is running the show. Therefore, activating 5% of our conscious awareness through traditional self-development will not lead to lasting change in our lives. Moreover, all of these self-help principles rely on one thing: that you can actually connect with the core of yourself and answer these questions honestly. We've already noticed that it's unlikely that you are able to tap into the unconscious 95%. Even still, are you being honest with the 5% that is within your conscious awareness? Let me be real with you. When's the last time you've been honest with yourself?

We all have moments in life where we are not being fully honest with ourselves. The problem arises when these moments cloud our true selves to the point that we no longer know who that person is. Then, we become like millions of other women, who now live the entirety of their lives for someone or something outside of themselves. And when we are not fully honest with ourselves, indecision creeps in.

Here's another inherent problem with all the personal development that's out there right now: we women are people pleasers, and we are highly vulnerable to our environment. As such, we are inherently biased by the instructor or teacher who is providing these insights. Without realizing it, we think, and maybe come to believe, that because Suzie Expert's life looks like X and because Suzie Expert is happy and healthy, then I must want Suzie Expert's life because I want to be happy and healthy, too. We read the books, follow the plans, and listen to the gurus because of one thing: we want to be like the gurus.

What do we do? We then go through course after course, conference after conference, and nothing really changes. If we're good students, we complete the course and reach the final destination. All the while, it's still not what we want. And, you guessed it, we don't feel any different. Why? Because we missed the first step. We missed the reconnection to the most important parts of ourselves. We then answer all these questions and proceed through life with an inherently flawed premise.

There's a hilarious MadTV bit from the early 2000s called "Stop It!" where Bob Newhart plays the role of a psychiatrist. His patient enters the room. He proceeds to tell her that he charges $5 for the first five minutes of the session and guarantees that the appointment will not last longer than five minutes. The patient begins to tell him about her fear of being buried alive in a box and her immense claustrophobia. He asks very few interpreting questions. Then, he gives his advice.

"STOP IT!" he yells. When she asks for clarification, he condescends, "S-T-O-P new word I-T! STOP. IT." She then tries to share some intimate information about her past and he pronounces, "STOP IT!" once more. There are some additional exchanges. Then, the patient says, "YOU STOP IT! I don't like this. I don't like this therapy at all." The clip ends with Newhart yelling, "STOP IT OR I'LL BURY YOU ALIVE IN A BOX!"

This text is clearly not doing justice to the humor of the clip, so I recommend you search on YouTube and watch it in full. For purposes of this book, understand that merely scolding at yourself to "Stop it" will do little to nothing to spur permanent change in your life. This is akin to the vast majority of personal development out there. Whether health and fitness goals or financial goals, you will likely not accomplish these goals by convincing your conscious mind. In order to "Stop It," you must uncover the unconscious drivers of your maladaptive behaviors in the first place and reconnect with the unconscious fragments of your heart in the process.

You can't expect to connect to your heart by reading one inspirational book or listening to one motivational speech. And the solution to the problem is not to *do* more. It's not to *be* more. It's not to *have* more.

There are thousands of millionaires these days who teach their plan, their strategy, or their solution to the problem. They assure you if you follow their path, then you can have their outcome: health, wealth, love (it pretty much all comes down to these three issues). And the promise is all the same: do more to feel better. Add a side hustle, make more money, read more books, workout longer, do more meal prep, go on more date nights, take more vacation. It's all about doing more.

I know, it can be subtle, but think about it. When is the last time you took one of these courses and sincerely felt any different? And if you did feel better, chances are it had nothing to do with the knowledge you were being given right in front of you. It had to do with the personal growth that you accomplished throughout the process. This is a matter of the *heart*, not the matter itself.

On the flip side, there are even rising gurus who will teach you to have less. Minimalism, Essentialism, The One Thing, Simple Living. While I am inclined to agree with these methods more than the former, they're still lacking. Why? Because they're still teaching you to *do* something to *feel* different. Getting rid of things, taking things off your to-do list, and simplifying your life are still about doing something different. I will admit: if you can get rid of physical clutter, sometimes it is easier to get to the heart of things, which is why I don't completely disagree with minimalism, and venture to practice simple living myself. Nonetheless, here's the biggest problem I see:

You are unhappy.

You begin searching outside of yourself for the answer.

You believe you find some answer to some detail of your life: diet, side hustle, business, education, husband, fashion, interior design, etc…

Small detail of life is solved. Maybe.

Life goes on.

Then, you are unhappy again.

You begin searching outside of yourself for the answer.

Again, you seem to find an answer to some small detail of your life.

Life goes on.

You begin to gain more awareness.

You realize that it's not about the small details. It's really about something bigger, something deeper.

Then, you buy into the "balanced life" phenomenon or the "simple living" phenomenon. Maybe both. At differing times in your life.

This new way of thinking may help for some time.

Until you realize you're not happy again.

The cycle of searching for answers outside of yourself until you are inevitably unhappy again continues until you're ping-ponging back and forth between different expert opinions, advice, or guidance. What you forget along the way: no one is like you. You cannot *think* your way *happy*, and you cannot *do* more when all you really want is to *feel* more.

I want to give you the solution to the problem so that you not only 1) know what things you ought to be doing to create the feeling that you're really after and 2) know how to actually *feel* when you are doing the things you choose to *do*.

Basically, most self-help books are the *what*. You already know the what. You know that you need to find the important stuff. You know you need to identify your priorities, live a "balanced life" (*eye roll*), live out your God-given purpose, or find clarity. You know that you should simplify your life and stop sweating the small stuff.

No one teaches the how. How do you find the most essential part of yourself? How do you find your heart?

4
If Not Self-Help, Then What?

You may now be disheartened by the notion that the *you* who you want to be appears somewhat outside of your reach. You are probably thinking, if 95% of me is not in my conscious control, then how can I even *be* me? You may also remember from junior high biology class that we cannot create new brain cells. When you kill brain cells from alcohol, drugs, or trauma, we do not build new cells. When we damage our spinal cord or suffer from a stroke or endure a neurodegenerative disease, we have permanent ailments, all because neurons do not replicate. So, you may assume that because we cannot create new brain cells, we cannot change our ingrained thoughts, feelings, and behaviors. While we cannot create new brain cells, there is hope. Neuroscience has come a long way in understanding the microscopic mechanisms of thoughts, behaviors, and emotions. More than that, the concept of neuroplasticity has transformed how we now view the brain and human behavior.

Neuroplasticity is the idea that our brains continue to change and evolve throughout our lives.[9] Researchers once assumed that because new neurons were not created over time,

35

our brain's development was halted as well, and thus, our habits and behaviors were largely determined from a young age. We now understand that our brains continue to develop well past the critical period of development in early childhood, not only microscopically but also in terms of large-scale cortical remapping.[10] That's a mouthful, but all it really means is creating a new road structure within the highway of your brain. Essentially, if you think of some ingrained habit, thought pattern, or behavior as an interstate highway, then in order to create change in your life, you need to shut down the interstate. Cortical remapping is the process that would lead you to the detours so that you can reach your final destination.

While large-scale changes (like redirecting traffic from several interstate highways) are much more frequent in our early years, it can still occur in stressful times in our lives. Research from patients who have suffered severe brain damage, like a stroke or traumatic brain injury, proves that large-scale remapping is possible. This explains why initial neurorehabilitation for stroke patients can predict recovery of neural pathways and help to build new neural networks.

Whether your brain has been damaged by external trauma or internal self-limiting forces, the only way I know to remap your heart is to uncover your unconscious and reconnect to the thoughts, desires, and beliefs that you have lost. There are many practices that prove to help you uncover your unconscious state, including meditation, prayer, and positive thinking. All practices begin with you becoming mindful of your conscious thoughts. In so doing, you then hold the power to form new roads in your brain. Once you are aware of your conscious thoughts, you can learn to challenge the unconscious states that led to these conscious thoughts in the process, or basically, why you formed the roads in the first place.

The traditional model of uncovering your unconscious is to spend years, decades even, in a kind of therapy founded by

Sigmund Freud known as psychodynamic therapy or insight-oriented therapy (or also known flippantly as "psychoanalysis"). Before I scare you away with mention of Freud, I assure you that psychodynamic therapy has progressed significantly over the past half century since Freud originally coined the philosophy.

Psychodynamic therapy has now been proven more effective than its more popular counterpart, cognitive behavioral therapy, in treating mild to moderate depression and anxiety, and it has been shown to be more effective than antidepressant medication alone.[11] Psychodynamic therapy is also beneficial in relieving chronic pain and other uncomfortable physical ailments common in psychiatric illness. The benefits increase the longer a patient is in therapy, but patients also continue to see improvement well past therapy has ended. All of these benefits are observed in as little as 12 weeks.

While psychodynamic therapy was originally isolated to long-term, intensive individual psychotherapy between a psychoanalyst and her patient, it has now been adapted for use in short-term time periods, as well as in group and couples therapy. And the classic image of a silent, veiled analyst sitting in a chair taking notes is no longer the norm.

Mind you, the traditional model of lying on the couch and talking for an hour while the therapist sits stoically can still be appreciated in some locales. But by and large, therapy has modernized, and even many pure psychoanalysts will use several therapy styles in a given setting. Moreover, the personality types of different therapists vary as much as the patients or clients whom they treat. One thing remains: one party (the individual) is seeking help from another party (the therapist). As therapy goes, the individual's role is to do the articulating and expressing, and the therapist's duty is to do the listening, uncovering, interpreting, and supporting.

This book turns the table on these presupposed roles. I will do the majority of the expressing while you will do the listening (i.e. reading) and interpreting. I will provide support, education, and encouragement. But I will also expect you to do the work of uncovering, interpreting, and processing.

The ultimate effect of psychotherapy is the ability to mobilize hope and other common factors for change. While I have emphasized that doing more is not the solution, I also know that you cannot live your life sitting in lotus pose all day. Therefore, it is not enough for me to help you merely uncover your unconscious without encouraging you to take action. In Part 4, I will finally walk you through how to live from the heart. Living from the heart is much akin to mobilizing hope. Living requires doing something, not merely feeling something. Living from the heart is practiced by reuniting with the most essential part of yourself and actively engaging with that part every day of your life.

It's Not About the Why

Popular opinion instructs you to "Start with your WHY." However, it may come as a shock to you that this goes against every psychodynamic philosophy I've ever learned. One of my early psychodynamic psychotherapy supervisors recited his "Therapy Pearls of Wisdom" frequently. The first Pearl was, don't ask your patient why, because they don't know. If you think about it, he is right. Why we say certain words or engage in certain behaviors is largely unconscious. You may give lip service to a superficial why based on insecurities, biases, or external judgment, but you are surely struggling to uncover the actual why.

As you will soon see, things are never as they seem. Likely, what you observe to be your problems at a conscious level are not the real problems at all. This is probably why your traditional self-help solutions have not worked either. You haven't been able to uncover the real problem in the first place. All you really can control is WHO? And that who is *you*.

I'll also make one thing clear: the only person you can control is yourself. It's a common complaint to want to place blame on others outside of yourself. While I empathize with your struggles, I also know that you cannot change another person. If you've ever tried to improve the habits of someone you love, you know that shame and nagging never work. Never. Ever. On the flip side, it takes more than positive affirmations and activism. At the heart of the matter, this is personal. And it starts with us. You. Me. In our own hearts.

I don't stand for excuses very well either. Some people just aren't happy. No matter how perfect their environments or circumstances, their attitudes never change. Unfortunately, many patients erroneously come to me with the sincere hope of "being fixed" as if they are just some bugged computer with a glitch that needs to be removed. But asking to be fixed is a less threatening way of asking to be healed, and that's really what we want: to be healed, rejuvenated, and to be made alive and whole again.

Being you is a longer, less sexy, less marketable road than being happy. Note: I said being happy, not feeling happy. Understand the difference. Happiness is a state of being. However, we often mistake happy for a fleeting state of emotion. Because it is a state of being, you have more control over it than you think. We can all choose to be happy. And I, for one, cannot make you happy. That's not what this book is about.

First, pull up your big girl panties and be ready to get to work. I know that accepting responsibility and acknowledging that you are the only one who can control the outcome is a challenging step for people, and it will likely become more challenging as you start to uncover the heart. I want you to bookmark this section and revisit it frequently.

I can't help anyone who doesn't want to be helped. So, I must ask, do you want help? Do you want to know yourself better? It's a serious question. At first glance, you may obviously answer yes. As you'll soon see, I want you to get in the habit of looking beyond the surface. In order to do that, identify all of the ways in which your life right now, and how you've been living your life right now, are good. Write down all of your reservations about change.

What to Expect

"Are you sure you want to do this?" my husband Travis commented as I was sitting in the car barreled over with nausea from a very winding drive in backwoods Kentucky to get to the Maker's Mark distillery.

"Yeah, sure, it'll be fun." I grimaced. Travis had traveled with me to my psychiatry residency interview at University of Louisville. I had no control over where Travis would be stationed next, so I applied to residency programs located near potential duty stations. Louisville is near Fort Knox, one Army post where he could have been stationed. I applied to the program and thankfully got an interview. Between my medical school class schedule and moving, this was the closest we were going to get to a Babymoon (you know, the last hurrah before your first baby is born). The tour of the Maker's Mark distillery was supposed to be a fun excursion on our vacation.

"We don't have to. We could just go back to the hotel or something. I mean, babe, you're pregnant." He had a point. I was 19 weeks pregnant, but being as it was my first pregnancy, I was barely showing. Nonetheless, going to a bourbon distillery hardly sounded enticing to a pregnant woman. Did I mention that the month before we had gone to Las Vegas? I spent the better part of that trip sleeping in our dreamy hotel room at *The Venetian*. I guess I'm a glutton for punishment.

"No, no, let's go. This will be fun. I've never been to a distillery. I'm better, I promise." I wasn't better. I was so exhausted, my feet were already swollen, and that car ride did me in. If I didn't have motion sickness before pregnancy, I definitely did now.

The distillery was beautifully decorated for Christmas and the crisp air made it enjoyable enough for me to forget my fatigue and nausea and actually learn a thing or two about bourbon. While I passed on the samples, I did enjoy a liqueur-filled chocolate at the end of the tour.

We made our way through the tour and learned how the grain was chosen and properly blended with water and then cooked and how yeast is managed. We learned about sour mash and the purpose of animal feed. We heard about the construction of the barrels and storage of the barrels, down to the filling of the bottles.

I wish I could recite all the glorious details of this process. To be honest, I'm still a little confused. What I did take away from the entire process is this: distillation takes *time*. A *long* time. Maker's Mark ages their bourbon a minimum of five years and nine months, and some are aged up to 20-30 years. Much like a good bottle of bourbon, distilling your heart will take time.

The quick fix scams are everywhere. Whether it's a diet or a get-rich-quick scheme or any other dramatic transformation, it takes time. Matters of the heart are no exception. Just think, you have spent a lifetime becoming the person you are today. Understanding yourself and making real change in your life will take time. How long will it take for you? I don't know. Everyone is different. Just as some women can get pregnant the first month they start trying, others require several months or years to conceive a baby.

Refining your heart is not an overnight process. As with most things in life, it is largely outside of your control. Sure, if you're beginning this journey with more self-awareness than most, you may be able to identify your heart sooner than others. In my experience though, three months is a pivotal time. In three months, you may start to gain awareness into the issues beyond the surface. This is a practice, though, and the practice of refining your heart is a lifelong process.

Anyone who has ever made a dramatic shift in her life can attest to the fact that the road to recovery is not linear. Failure, or at least perceived failure, is bound to occur along the way. It takes the average smoker nine times to quit smoking.[12] It takes seven attempts for a woman to leave an abusive relationship, according to The National Domestic Violence Hotline.[13] It takes an average of five treatments until an eating disorder patient enters recovery. [14]

While you may not be recovering from an addiction, you are recovering from a lifetime of habits and coping mechanisms that are largely outside of your conscious state of awareness. You have been at war with yourself for a long time. Battle wounds of the heart will not be healed overnight. Value progress over perfection. Know that this work will never end. That may sound overwhelming in and of itself. Honor the process. You will have highs and lows. With awareness of your hurts and weaknesses, you will better handle the daily challenges that come your way. You will learn to identify the root issues and chisel away the details holding you back.

In Part 2, I will present my framework of the HEART. This is a framework that I crafted to help you uncover yourself. In Part 3, I put HEART into practice in your daily life. After listening to the same issues from my patients and taking inventory of my own life, I methodically chose particular subjects to be the bulk of discussion matter. I share personal stories, as well as patient stories, by way of example and an opportunity to connect. In Part 3, you can go through the chapters in order or flip to the sections that resonate most with you. I hope at some point you will make it through each chapter though.

You will not achieve lasting change, success, freedom, or joy merely by following the latest 12 module plan to a dream life. To make radical change requires radical effort. While I don't always agree with the latest personal development trend, marketing guru, or health coach, we can all agree on this: to kill it in life, love, and business, you have to be you.

While I cannot give you the steps to happiness or wealth, I can give you the steps to uncover your heart. I can also show you all the stumbling blocks along the way. Hopefully, by unveiling the burdens and removing the barriers, you have an easier time of reconnecting with who you are and what is truly important in your life.

I can give you the tools to uncover what's underneath, to break down the barriers and confront the real issues. The reason you are discontent in life, love, career, or family is because you are holding onto something deeper underneath. Until you reveal your heart, confront your deep truths, and process your pain, you will remain burdened by obscene, unknown forces, and you will continue seeking answers outside of yourself.

I don't have all the answers, and I definitely can't predict the future, let alone *your* future. But I do know that if you want to succeed in your business, improve your marriage, or reclaim your health, you need a different approach. You need insight into your unconscious mind. That's what I'm going to give you. Because I believe we have it inside all of us to live a rich, fulfilling life. This book is only one step, perhaps the first step, in your journey. This is not an overnight fix. The more you can acknowledge your unconscious, the easier it is to live consciously. You will be on your way to let *your* heart out and be unapologetically you.

5
Accepting Who You Really Are

"Hey Karen, would you mind covering for me?" I asked sheepishly. I knew I wasn't supposed to leave my patients in the middle of the day, but I had to make it to my psychiatrist appointment.

"Yeah, sure, it's no problem. Where are you going by the way? In case Dr. N asks, that is." She barely looked up at me. She was still typing her notes for the day. Good, she couldn't see how nervous I was.

Why was I so nervous? "I have a doctor's appointment," I said under my breath as I was gathering my things. I placed my phone and pager on the desk in front of Karen. I took off my white coat in lieu of my winter coat. I grabbed my purse and walked to leave the call room when—

"Hey Stefani?" Karen questioned. She abruptly looked up from the computer and turned her head to face me.

"Yeah?" I kept walking, not looking her in the face. I knew I might break down in tears if she looked at me. Karen was one of my closest confidants in residency. She also had the incredible power of reading me like a book. She was a good psychiatrist.

"Is everything okay?" she probed.

I stopped in my tracks. All of a sudden, my legs did not work. I could feel her concerned eyes on my back.

"Stefani, I can tell something is off about you. I'm just worried, that's all." I hadn't worked alongside her all year, but now that we were on a new rotation together, we had seen each other every day for the past two weeks. I should've known it was a matter of time before she picked up on my suffering.

"No," I mumbled under my breath. I turned around. "No, I'm not okay." I spoke up. I still couldn't look her in the face, but my voice was steady.

"What's going on? Tell me what I can do to help." She sounded so sincere. I believed every word, even though I knew I wasn't at a place to accept her help. Not yet.

"It's okay, I'm seeing someone... a professional," I stammered. Why was this so hard to get out? "My doctor's appointment is actually with a psychiatrist... I actually started taking medication last month." I managed to get it out. It felt so good to say it out loud. Outside of my mom and Travis, Karen was the first person I told that I was getting help for my postpartum depression.

"Oh, that's great!" she jumped out of her chair and nearly knocked me over in a bear hug. "I mean, not great that you're not feeling well, but I'm so happy you're getting help. We were actually starting to get worried." She pulled away from me and held me at arm's length.

"We?"

"Yeah, well, me and Bruce, we knew you weren't okay. We just didn't know how to talk to you."

I thought I hid it pretty well.

"Really?" I was still perplexed. *Why hadn't anyone talked to me sooner? I would've listened. Wouldn't I?*

"Yeah, well, it takes one to know one. Haven't I told you about my experience with postpartum depression after Helen was born?"

No, I definitely would have remembered. "Uh, I don't remember."

"Oh, it was awful. I was so traumatized, ya know, after her premature birth and stay in the NICU. I guess I could see myself in you these past few weeks. Call it a sixth sense, but I could tell you might be suffering from the same thing I was." Karen was always so honest and real with her own struggles. I will always be profoundly grateful for her transparency.

"By the way, don't worry. I won't say anything to Dr. N. Doctor-patient confidentiality, you know?" she winked at me. "Now, go on. Get out of here. Don't miss your appointment." She shooed me out.

I smiled as I walked out of the call room. In that moment, I didn't feel so alone.

In our suffering, it is easy to feel isolated. In fact, the most comforting words in the English language can be *me too*. I want you to know you are not alone. I hear enough stories to know that suffering is more the norm than the exception. Whether or not you suffer from postpartum depression or some other mental illness, we all struggle to feel worthy. It's no wonder when we are inundated by the same prevailing message from society: *you are not good enough*.

At the heart of my postpartum depression, all of my emotions boiled down to one resounding feeling that I wasn't good enough. I wasn't a good enough mother or a good enough doctor or a good enough wife or a good enough friend. I kept trying to chase some fantasy version of myself. In order to feel enough as we are, we need to stop pursuing the fantasy version of ourselves and learn to accept the reality of what is.

Accept Reality

In every romance novel, movie, musical, or play, there is the priceless moment where the beautiful ingénue and the dashing prince meet for the first time. In the theater world, it's called your "meet cute." For entertainment, this word says it all. Meeting a crush or a handsome man is usually cute. There's some flirting involved. If it's a Danielle Steel novel, there's likely third-base action in the first meeting. Sparing all the lush details, there are always positive vibes. Unless, of course, it's the "can't-stand-you-but-then-I-fall-in-love-with-you" diatribe. And then, the meet cute is still, well, cute, because we love the great friction that comes from a more "real life" meeting. Is it real life though? Sadly, if Hollywood or romance novelists actually talked about real life, they would only get a yawn and negative reviews because it "didn't end the way I thought it would." They'd probably go out of business.

One of the most popular reality TV show couples, Chip and Joanna Gaines of *Fixer Upper*, share in their book that when the camera crew came to film their sizzle reel (what would be used as a pitch to the network for whether they would get the show or not), they were utterly boring. The camera crew followed them around for a few days only to get the "everyday life," which wasn't going to cut it. It wasn't until a dramatic goof by Chip that the production team saw a hit show. While I love the Gaines, I also know that I cannot see their entire lives in just one hour of *Fixer Upper*. And though they are probably more genuine than other reality TV shows, there is still significant staging and preparation that goes into play to get all the heartwarming moments of each episode.

Want to hear about *my* reality? Truth time. As I write this, I am sitting in my hodgepodge of a spare room filled with Army gear, storage, books, a workout bench, dumbbells, a camera and lighting equipment, framed pictures stacked on the floor, a dozen toys, and loose papers strewn on the floor. And this is the cleanest room in my house right now. You see, I've become a bit of a messy woman over past couple years. According to my mom, "messy women have good sex," so I guess I got that going for me. Oh, did I mention that it's 5 am on a Sunday? My anniversary to be exact. (*Love you, babe!*)

Real life isn't pretty. It's not smoke and mirrors of Hollywood lore. It's not a Pinterest-worthy farmhouse-designed home. (For the record, even Joanna Gaines talks about letting her house go after having kids in *The Magnolia Story*. Great read by the way.) Real life isn't a meet cute. Some parts are really ugly, others are beautiful, and most are mundane. Finding luxury in the mundane is the joy.

You likely have spent so much time living for others, caught up in your thoughts or emotions, that peeling it all away now leaves you raw and vulnerable. It is in this vulnerability that you can come to be authentically you and make real change in your life. If you're like most of us, your heart is bruised and broken, covered in rust and grime, with maybe some graffiti print of harsh words or traumatic language from your past. You're missing parts of your heart, theft from nameless bystanders. Your heart is misshapen and dull. Challenging outside influences, thoughts, emotions, and beliefs is not easy. The hardest work of all starts now.

Accept Brokenness

We're conditioned from a young age to associate "broken" with "bad." I remember dropping a bowl when I was a little girl and getting the stern look from my parents. Without much thought, I picked up the pieces of the bowl and put it swiftly in the trash. In these subtle instances, we come to associate brokenness with trash. Like the shattered bowl, many of our hearts have been shattered. Instead of looking to repair the bowl, we want to throw our hearts in the trash and reach for some cheap substitute. From a young age, we imprint a sense of shame with brokenness.

In order to avoid this feeling of shame, we turn to cheap remedies. The statistics don't lie. More than a third of adolescents regularly use illicit drugs.[15] The opioid epidemic is prevalent. Drug use has escalated since 2007, and alcohol dependence has become normalized. Worse, it's estimated that only 1% of those suffering from alcohol and substance use disorders are actually receiving the treatment that they need.

Along with substance use disorders, mental illness is on the rise. More than half of all adults experience mental illness at some point in their lives. Almost 20% of new mothers will experience postpartum depression within the first year of baby's life.[16] And it's estimated that less than half of those moms will get the help they need.

Now, you may not have a drug problem or a serious mental illness, but we are all broken in some way, shape, or form. Chances are you have your own drug of choice. Whether through destructive relationships, work-a-holism, perfectionism, or the like, you avoid your brokenness through alternate means.

Embracing our brokenness is pivotal to continue with this work. In Japan, there is a beautiful art called *kintsugi*. In practice, they take broken objects, most commonly pottery, and through the repair process, they weave in metallic paints of gold, silver, or platinum. Breakage and repair becomes part of the beautiful history of the object, rather than something to dispose of or disguise. The end product is often more luxurious than the beginning product, and each product is unique in its own right.

So many patients spend years in therapy, and, in their words, they "never get better." It's because you can't talk away your brokenness, but you can *embrace* your brokenness as a beautiful piece of art.

Acknowledge the Complexity

When we embrace our brokenness, we can come to acknowledge our own complexity. We are never one thing. Life is about contrasts and contradictions. We are each, in our own unique way, a walking paradox. I love flowers, but I hate gardening. I love nature, but I hate camping. I prefer dresses to pants, but I'm hardly high-fashioned. I love red wine, but I hate a poor night's sleep. I like nightclubs, but I cannot stay awake past 10 pm. I like the beach, but I hate sand. I love cooking, but I don't like following a recipe. I like road trips, but I don't want to be in a car.

We all remember studying the complex characters from the required literature reading of our school days, yet we rarely see reason to accept the subtle nuances of ourselves. We live in a linear, black-and-white world. We wrongly attempt to place not only ourselves in boxes but also those around us. So, we make labels and stereotypes and cliques. This is our effort to make sense of the multidimensional complexities of our hearts.

To begin to notice and accept these complexities is paramount to fully coming to terms with who and what we are. We can then accept that just because we display certain traits in one environment doesn't mean that we must be that person in every environment. Personality tests and strengths assessments notoriously bring out this contrasted thinking in us. When we acknowledge certain strengths within us, we then want to define our lives by these strengths. We seek career paths and romantic partners and social experiences based on these analyses. All the while, we forget to acknowledge the myriad of nuances that arise within very broad personality exams.

Friends and family used to tell me I was "rough around the edges." I think we are all rough around the edges as we are finding our groove in the world. Our prickly edges are our insecurity or lack of confidence in given situations and circumstances. Until we can freely allow ourselves to be just as we are, we will continue to lead with our unpolished self.

Embrace the Imperfection

Along with understanding the complexities of our heart, we must embrace our imperfection. Fear of imperfection is one of the most common fears for women. I know the fear all too well. I lived much of my life as a perfectionist. I thought an activity was not worth my time unless I could be the best at it, and I competed to be the best at everything I did.

Ironically, the pursuit of perfectionism stems from a level of high achievements from a young age. Our developing brains become conditioned to success. As we grow and mature, it is impossible to keep up the same level of success that we had as young girls. We play in more competitive leagues. We face more talented opponents. We will naturally not be able to hold up the same stamina we had from the wonder years. While our driven, competitive nature serves us well in sports and childhood activities, adulthood is not framed around perfection.

Paradoxically, the same level of success from a young age that may have doomed us to a never-ending pursuit of perfectionism was likely also the same thing that developed a secure, confident sense of self. Having small wins in childhood does help us develop confidence into adulthood. But, over time, we can become dissatisfied with small wins. This inability to acknowledge our own greatness can lead us to constantly search for the unobtainable perfectionism.

Motherhood especially brings to rise mass fears of perfectionism. In my online program, Push Past Postpartum™, I help postpartum moms with mood and anxiety disorders. I'm told by clients that one of the most pivotal lessons in the course is about breaking down the fantasy version of ourselves and embracing imperfection. We not only want to be the best version of ourselves, but we assume that if we are not perfect, then we will ruin our child's lives in some way, shape, or form. But there's no such thing as a perfect mother. Motherhood, in particular, is more like "50 Shades of Imperfection."

This has been a particularly challenging skill for me to learn. The journey goes like this: you pursue perfectionism in all areas of your life, you observe that this is unsustainable so you choose to only do things that you are perfect at, so you avoid any activities that you may not be perfect at. Eventually, you come to acknowledge your realistic limitations, you engage in things that you are not perfect at for the sake of joy and sanity, and you give up the pursuit of fantasy. When we can acknowledge our limitations, we can escape the futuristic fantasy and finally begin living in the here and now.

Accept Your Weaknesses

While perfectionism may be an overarching dogma, our weaknesses arise in specific parts of our lives. Accepting our weaknesses is a necessary next step in overcoming perfectionism and challenging underlying fears and limiting beliefs.

Consider that the more flaws you have, the more relatable you are. No one wants to be around someone whom they view as unapproachable. Politicians will spend millions of dollars on consultants so that they can appear more down-to-earth. Usually, this requires an appropriate level of transparency regarding past mistakes and failures. Similarly, *Lifetime* movies are not based on picture-perfect lives. Protagonists in bestselling novels are never without character flaws. We like hearing the trials and struggles. Character flaws and weaknesses make us human. Moreover, you are a lot more fun to be around when you let your weaknesses shine. People who are open with their weaknesses can take life less seriously. I've never met a seemingly perfect person who I actually enjoyed being around.

This practice is about more than just being transparent about your weaknesses. These days, it's actually become in vogue to share your life's drama and trials to your entire social media feed. While I'm all about honesty and acknowledgment of your weaknesses, I also recommend protecting your Achilles heel. If we have not fully accepted our weaknesses, we can easily put ourselves in a vulnerable state. Be cautious in sharing your vulnerability until you have done the work. Our inner monologue will seek to attack our weaknesses, and unconsciously we will make up for our weaknesses through overcompensation.

For example, a patient of mine admitted to me that she didn't want to return to work after the birth of her son. She then immediately retorted, "But I mean, I don't have anything against working mothers." On the outside, this kind of comment could be overlooked as just an overly sensitive, conscientious mother (obviously, she knew that I was a working mother, so maybe she was trying not to offend me). Yet, she missed the boat. She avoided the acknowledgment of her weakness: she is still uncertain about being a stay-at-home mother and remains ever-judgmental of her decision to be home with her son.

Of course, our weaknesses can be more concrete in nature as well. I, for one, am not great at arts and crafts. This is a recurring theme in my life. As such, I often lament that I do not do a lot of arts and crafts projects with my kids. Usually, soon after I share this fact, I make it known that I am a working mother or that I prefer something else instead of arts and crafts. Clearly, I feel insecure about my lack of hands-on projects with my kids, so this is my weakness. I can easily come to accept this about myself (as I have) without the added banter of requiring an explanation for my said weakness.

Identify Your Strengths

The great thing about being able to accept our weaknesses is that we are one step closer to acknowledging and compounding

54

our strengths. We can think of our strengths as the flipside of our weaknesses, two sides of the same coin. My outspoken, opinionated nature has been a real hindrance at times in my life. It's also my best asset. I consider myself brave, and—daresay—impulsive, which sometimes gets me into trouble. At the same time, I would most certainly not be where I am today without challenging the status quo from a young age and fearlessly taking many leaps in my life.

The problem lies when we continue to view our strengths as weaknesses or when we are trapped in an environment where our strengths are indeed weaknesses. For instance, if my job required a more reserved, subservient nature, I would not excel. If I was trying to make a relationship work with someone who did not value my expressiveness, I would be miserable.

The key is to name your strengths, which again is usually some rendition of your weaknesses. Then, find ways in which you can utilize your strengths on a daily basis. Seek opportunities or avenues that transform your weaknesses into strengths. Being able to live within our strengths will easily connect us to our hearts. Please keep in mind that while your strengths can be a large window into your heart, it is not your heart exclusively.

It is easy to identify ourselves by our strengths, but make sure to understand them from a current vantage point. You will change and morph over time. With any given change or adjustment in your life, your strengths may adapt. The strengths you may have had and identified with as a child may no longer be your allies. This is an ongoing evaluation, a process that never ends. Being able to shed old strengths in favor of new advancements is what will continue to serve you on this heart-centered journey.

Accept the Changes

As we accept our multidimensional character, we must also accept that life, and how we show up in that life, will also undoubtedly change over time. You are likely not the same person that you were as a child or even five years ago. And you definitely are not the same person today that you will be ten years from now. Based on the external changes happening to us, we will undoubtedly change on the inside. This is all to be expected.

For me, I never dreamed of being an Army wife. My parents still live in the home that I grew up in. With the exception of three months studying abroad in Europe in college, I spent my entire life in Texas until I was seven months pregnant with Kate. We moved cross country to Washington, D.C. in the middle of winter. Within a few short months, I faced several changes. I completed a research internship at the Centers for Disease Control (CDC), I graduated medical school, I finished my Masters of Public Health degree, my husband started a demanding new job, our dog required double-knee surgery and doggie rehab (yes, it's a thing), my dad had a stroke, Kate was born via C-section, and I began my internship in psychiatry.

I look back on that time now in awe that I made it out alive. Yet the next year of my life would prove to be even more challenging. In many respects, it was the worst year of my life. I worked every single holiday. Every. Single. Holiday. I didn't travel home for over a year. I had a newborn. I was working 60-80-hour work weeks. My husband and I were geographically separated at times. I had no friends or family nearby. It's no wonder why I suffered from postpartum depression.

Any individual who goes through that many changes in such a short period of time will undoubtedly experience massive change of heart. I no longer had time for superficial junk in my life. Slowly, the details of life were forgotten. I am now grateful for this challenging time of my life. It changed my heart for the better.

However, my hope for you is that you don't need catastrophe to strike for you to forgo the details of life and reconnect to your truest self. We cannot always control the changes that happen to us, but we can control how we respond to these changes and whether or not we change as an individual. It's not realistic to assume that you will remain the same person forever. We will change over time. We *must* change over time. Our personalities will change. Our relationships will change. Our strengths and weaknesses will change. Change is a good thing. If you are not changing, then you are not growing. Like any change, it can be anxiety-provoking. Even with good changes, we usually challenge the resistance.

This is important to note, because it is easy to be driven by who you want to be or who you used to be rather than who you are right now. But let me tell you something: only when you can fully embrace who you are right now will you ever be able to make any meaningful change in who you are, if that is what you desire. My hope is that you can control the changes of who you are, despite the unexpected changes happening around you, and that you can stand true in who you are, despite the chaos around you.

PART 2

Draw Your HEART

I want to be me
More than anything else
More than things
More than stuff
More than trophies at hand
More than people
More than friends
More than love on my heart
I want to be me
More than me

-Stefani Reinold

Over the next five chapters, I will introduce you to the HEART method. Through stories and examples, I will guide you into a deeper understanding of your unconscious mind. I weave in exercises throughout, known as "hearts and crafts." Each exercise builds on itself. For the most benefit, I recommend you complete this entire section without interruption.

It may seem cumbersome to engage in "hearts and crafts" projects. Please know that I would never waste your time. I molded this method for you based on my clinical experience treating more than a thousand patients, as well as my academic knowledge of the unconscious mind. After seeing such significant benefits, I now recommend this method for you. It will then serve as the foundation for the application in Parts 3 and 4.

Requirements:
- An open mind
- A desire to know yourself better
- Safe environment

Time:
- One to two hours, uninterrupted, best accomplished during baby's naptime or after your kids' bedtime

Supplies:
- This book
- Timer
- Pen
- Crayons, markers, or colored pencils
- Highlighter or marking pen
- Blank paper
- Coloring page*
- Stickers, glitter, other artistic elements (optional)
- Glass of Wine (optional, but highly recommended)

Instructions:

To begin, find a safe space where you will not be interrupted. I say safe, not necessarily quiet. It doesn't matter where you are—home, coffee shop, work—as long as you feel secure in that moment and you have privacy. Sit in a comfortable chair, preferably not a bed or anywhere that evokes drowsiness. Make sure you have a sturdy writing surface. Gather your supplies within reach. Open your mind. Dive in.

*You can download your free coloring page at letyourheartoutbook.com

6
Here and Now

Any kind of change must begin with becoming aware of the here and now. In fact, most mental illness sufferers live the majority of their lives outside of the realm of reality. While the severe cases of psychosis literally live in a world run by their delusions and hallucinations, most cases of depression and anxiety function in either dwelling on the past or obsessing about the future. Author James Altucher in his book, *Choose Yourself*, calls this "time traveling." The more we time travel, the more miserable we become. You may not hear voices like a schizophrenic patient does, but you likely spend the majority of your lifetime traveling in and out of touch with your current reality. The thing is, we can only control the here and now, and dwelling on the past or obsessing about the future will do nothing to create change in our lives.

"Savannah, it's okay, you're safe," I said calmly. Even though I hadn't slept more than a couple of hours last night on call, helping patients always filled my heart.

"Wh... wh... where am I? Who are you? What am I doing here?" She jerked her limbs, abruptly pulling her blanket over her body. Her breathing quickened. Her eyes glared into me like I was some abuser. Her hands formed fists. She was ready to protect herself. *She thinks I'm her mother*, I thought.

"Savannah, I'm Dr. Reinold, your psychiatrist. You had a bad dream. Do you know where you are right now?" My tone was neutral. I had to stay calm. Trauma patients are so highly charged with emotion that it's important to level the environment.

"Who? Wait... what..." She kept looking at me sternly, but with less hatred. She relaxed her fists. Her breathing calmed.

"I know it's scary. Can you tell me what you see around you?" Bringing someone down from a flashback or nightmare can be challenging. It requires helping a patient focus on the here and now.

"I... I... I see you..." she stammered. Her eyes widened as she took in the surroundings around her.

"Good..." I encouraged.

"And... I see the gray wall... I see my white blanket."

"You're doing great, Savannah," I comforted. Savannah was a well-known patient of mine. She had a significant trauma history: sexual abuse from her father, impregnated by her father, gave birth to a stillborn baby, medical complications of Type 1 diabetes, and further sexual abuse and assault from subsequent men. She was also familiar with the common technique of grounding.

Grounding is a practice for trauma patients in order to help them become aware of their current state of affairs. When trauma patients begin to experience flashbacks, the memory itself can feel very real to them. It's important to come down to reality. Grounding is getting in touch with all five senses in your current reality.

"What do you hear?"

"I hear your voice... the nurses are talking in the hallway." Her voice was calmer, breathing less shallow. She had now propped herself up in her bed on her elbows. She had taken her gaze from me and was now surveying the room.

"That's so good. What do you feel touching your body?"

"The bed... the blanket."

"Do you smell anything?"

"It smells like hand sanitizer," she scrunched her nose and looked at me with a grin. We both chuckled a little. I knew she was coming out of it.

"How do you feel now?" I implored.

"I'm a little better. I'm just tired. Can I rest now?" She was lying down in bed.

"Yes, you can rest now." I looked at my watch. 3:32 am. The adrenaline rush was wearing off. I was hoping to get a little rest in the call room as well. I began to walk out of the patient room when—

"And Dr. Reinold?" she called out.

"Yes?"

"Thank you." My heart melted. As difficult as my job can be, I love knowing that I can truly make a difference in someone's life.

Now, you may or may not live in your flashbacks like a trauma patient does, but you likely are not living in the present moment either. Let's review the average morning of a typical working mother.

5:00 am: Wake up. Hit snooze. Roll over in bed. Try to go back to sleep. Either insomnia kept you awake last night or baby woke you up multiple times.

5:10 am: Second alarm. Pick up phone. Check Facebook. No notifications? Check Instagram. Yay! More hearts. Now, I'll be in a good mood.

5:20 am: Get out of bed. Use restroom.

5:25 am: Stumble to kitchen. Turn on coffee maker, boil

tea kettle, grab a Red Bull, mainline caffeine straight through an IV. Take your pick.

5:30 am: Sit on couch. Try to read, journal, or meditate. That's what all the gurus say. Mind races to daily to-do list and all the shoulda, coulda, wouldas.

5:40 am: Grab a pen and paper to write down all of the gibberish in your brain. Proceed to forget everything that was in your brain.

5:45 am: Return to bed. Hubby still sleeping. How can he still be sleeping? Seriously… Check Facebook again. Still no notifications. Oh, but it is me and my cousin's friendsversary today. Cool, when did Facebook start doing that? No. Put. The. Phone. Down.

5:55 am: Put on workout clothes. If you can't sleep, might as well do something productive before kids wake up.

6:00 am: *Waaaaahhhhhh waaaahhhh…* oh, baby is awake. Standing up, crying in his crib. Maybe he'll go back to sleep.

6:05 am: *Maaaahhhh—ummmmm!!!* Only toddlers can make mom two syllables. Well, I guess the baby woke up the toddler. Mom on duty begins now.

6:10 am: Look over at husband. Still sleeping. *STILL…*

6:15 am: Bring baby a bottle or nurse him. Put Disney channel on for toddler.

6:30-7:00am: Attempt to put on something decently civil for work that does not have spit up stains on it.

7:00 am: Give hubby kiss as he heads out the door for work. When did he wake up? I totally missed him. Stealth mode. How can I get that superpower?

7:05 am: Make breakfast for kids while preparing lunches.

7:15 am: Get kids dressed.

7:30 am: Realize you haven't eaten breakfast yet. Chug a protein smoothie or eat your kids' leftovers.

7:45 am: Leave the house. Drop the kids off at school or daycare, forgetting at least one thing you or your kids needed today.

After work, the typical evening isn't much better:

5:00 pm: Leave work at five on the dot in order to race through traffic to pick up kids.

5:30 pm: Pick up kids barely on time. Yes, no late fee charges this time.

5:45 pm: Get home. Immediately put on cartoon for toddler. Feed baby.

6:00 pm: Greet husband as he comes through the door, perplexed by the once neat home that now appears as though a tornado touched down in a span of 15 minutes flat.

6:05 pm: Wonder what to have for dinner. Pour glass of wine while contemplating.

6:10 pm: Eventually settle on leftovers, frozen, steamable veggie pack, or George Foreman-inspired chicken. Or peanut butter. Peanut butter is always a viable dinner option.

6:20 pm: Make small talk over dinner while toddler puts a fight akin to Custard's Last Stand against said dinner options.

6:30 pm: Give in to said toddler and make macaroni and cheese for dinner. I know she'll eat that.

6:45 pm: Change into pajamas, because hey #comfortfirst

7:00 pm: Give kids bath.

7:10 pm: Leave kids in bath to check social media. Did I get more likes today? More followers?

7:15 pm: Ignore kids crying to get out of bathtub so that you can finish using the restroom all by yourself.

7:20 pm: Save children from bath. Lotion them down, brush their teeth, and get ready for bed.

7:30 pm: Tuck children into bed.

7:40 pm: Return to connect with husband.

8:00 pm: Continue working on side hustle but instead get sidetracked by social media black hole.

9:00 pm: Retreat to bedroom. Try to plan next day. Write out hopes and dreams. Pray. Read Bible study.

9:30 pm: Fall asleep.

Of course, I am exaggerating a little bit here. And jokes aside, most husbands are pretty great when you know how to enlist their services. Honestly, though, this example is not far from the truth. The consistent thread across many of our lives is this: your time is spent doing, thinking, or being something or someone other than yourself for something or someone outside of yourself.

Confession time: my wedding day was not the happiest day of my life. Not because I was marrying the wrong person; I adored (and still adore) my husband. Not because I felt ugly or unworthy in some way; I felt like the most beautiful woman in the world. Not because people didn't show up; I was incredibly grateful for so many friends, family, and wedding guests who would share this special day with me. Not even because there was family drama; my family was supportive, attentive, and encouraging the entire day.

All things considered, my wedding day was spectacular. The venue was a quaint, shabby chic winery. The ceremony was held outside with the backdrop of the grape vines adorned by delicate flowers. My bridesmaids were wonderful, the flower girls were adorable, the groomsmen were great. Guests received a complimentary glass of wine before the ceremony began. The ceremony was beautiful. We mingled with all of our guests in a receiving line before enjoying a relaxing, cocktail style reception with a live jazz band, buffet, and the most delicious wedding cake that I've ever eaten. I wore my grandmother's wedding gown for the ceremony and my modern yet vintage mermaid dress for the reception. All the elements—decor, flowers, food, and atmosphere—were the perfect blend of classic and modern. Traditional meets progressive, just like me. But something was missing.

My heart.

I held it together well and most of my friends still to this day tell me how "relaxed" I was on my wedding day. While I did not feel anxious or rushed, I also was not present. I had no heart on my wedding day. I was trapped inside my head, drowning in thoughts and to-dos and what-ifs and shoulds. I forgot to live and enjoy this once-in-a-lifetime day. I don't believe in regrets, but I am saddened by this bleak reality. I'm thankful for a wonderful, forgiving husband who, despite a crazed first day of our life together, remains my foothold when I need him most.

While many brides share my sentiments on their wedding day, we women often go through life with the same hustle and bustle of our wedding day. We assign the same amount of priority to the small stuff in life as the big stuff. Based on the anxiety level of a woman, you would imagine that it was her wedding day every day. The truth is: most women live their lives trapped in their thoughts. In fact, chances are, you have been doing it so long that you don't even know how to turn it off.

Intellectualization is a common mental attitude defense mechanism. Intellectualization, in particular, is so common that we no longer see it for what it is: a defense. Meaning, it's not real. Meaning, you're protecting yourself from something or avoiding something. Intellectualization is a defense mechanism where thoughts and reasoning are used to avoid or cover up an unconscious conflict. Because unconscious conflicts often bring up pain and discomfort, intellectualization is the avenue for which you can escape from these painful emotions and stressful events.

Intellectualization can be incredibly helpful in crisis situations. Obviously, if your child is hurt or you're in a car accident, I don't want you wallowing in a puddle of tears. Your thoughts will drive you to care for your child or to ensure your safety. But when we spend most of our time living in our head, that's when it becomes problematic. Not only are your thoughts holding you back from feeling your emotions, challenging your beliefs, and mending your heart, but your thoughts are also lying to you.

An average woman has between 50,000-70,000 thoughts per day, and 98% of those thoughts are the exact same thoughts playing themselves over and over. And over. If you're hearing 50,000 lies a day, it's no wonder you are stuck living in the same patterns of your life. As you'll soon find out, your thoughts can be a powerful window into your heart. Until you train your mind to see beyond your superficial thoughts, you will continue repeating the same lies to yourself. As a result, you will remain stuck in your current habits and behaviors.

The foundation of the HEART method begins with gaining awareness of the here and now. Think of this exercise as grounding for your heart.

Hearts and Crafts
Free Association Writing

. . . .

- ♥ Grab your pen and blank pieces of paper.
- ♥ Set an alarm for a period of time between 10 to 15 minutes.
- ♥ Then, write. Do not stop moving your hand. Write whatever comes to your mind no matter how ridiculous or annoying or crazy it is. Repeat yourself. Write illegibly. Write gibberish. The point is to get past the "pretty" cohesive thoughts and to uncover the "dirty" disorganized thoughts within us.
- ♥ When the timer goes off, stop writing.
- ♥ Grab your coloring page.
- ♥ Review your freestyle writing.
- ♥ Circle or highlight important elements:
  Key words
  Names of people you mention more than once
  Contradictory phrases or conflicts
- ♥ Write these words inside your heart on your coloring page.

Share your heart on Instagram with the hashtag #letyourheartout

If you've seen the movie *Inception*, you remember the scene where the dream architect Ariadne (Ellen Page) is walking down the street with Dom Cobb (Leonardo DiCaprio). As they walk, Dom explains what Ariadne is viewing and refers to the current state as the projection of his unconscious. As they continue walking, Ariadne begins experimenting with the physics and dimensions of the environment around her by walking upside down, creating mirrors, and imagining a parallel world.

While I won't be asking you to create some alternate universe, my work is to get you to uncover thoughts that are outside of your conscious state of reality. Put another way, writing your thoughts is akin to a flat, two-dimensional representation of your mind. To add additional dimensions, we need to activate new parts of our brain.

Example:
I want to speak and share my story in the hopes of making a difference. I want to make a difference. I want to change the experience for others behind me. I want to change for my children and for their children. I want more love, less hate, less indifference in the world. More honesty and more real and raw conversations. I want people to be able to share and connect. Connection is what it is all about for me. I would have back-to-back, 1:1 conversations.

In this example, I would highlight the words "want," "difference," "connection," and "conversations."

Next, mark all of the people that you mention more than once. Write their names on your paper.

Example:

I'm glad my grandma is going to get to come. God's been so good to me. God is good. Probably too good to me. My grandma is so great. My dad's heart attack. Adulthood is not the version we hear as kids. I hope I'm doing a good job explaining things to my kids. I want to have fun. It'll be fun to go out this weekend. I want a date night, not family night. Does that make me a bad person?

In this example, I would mark the people as grandma, God, dad, and kids.

Last, review any contradictory phrases or conflicts in your writing.

Example:

I wish I felt caught up. I only feel rushed. Hurried by the overwhelming forces. I'm so chill though. I'm amazed that life is this good. Why is it this good? I'm pretty blessed in life. I never feel good enough though. Why is that? Why oh why? My daughter was bad today. I can't believe her sometimes. She has such a good head on her shoulders but sometimes, she's just crazy. I'm shocked at how relaxed she seems sometimes and other times, she's out of control.

In this example, I made a note of "rushed vs. chill," "good vs. bad," "crazy/out of control vs. relaxed."

Review your notes. Mark down any themes that consistently arise. Record these on your coloring page. For now, just write the words on your coloring page. We will continue to add color and dimension to your heart over the next few chapters.

7

*E*mbrace Your Emotions

When I was a kid, my older brother and I would go to Putt-Putt Golf and Games, a common hot spot for birthday parties, school fundraisers, and social gatherings. We would spend hours on various games, winning as many tickets as we could. With our tickets, we would carefully pick out a prize. My favorite prizes were usually candy or colored pencils. One particular time, I remember being enamored by the neon-colored Chinese finger knots. They had a sheen of glitter on the surface and glowed in the dark. I thought they looked so cool. When I saw another kid buy one with his tickets, I knew I wanted the same one for myself.

I gave all of my earnings over to the cashier and was given two knots: one neon pink and one neon purple. I quickly slid it over my two index fingers, as I had seen the other boy do with his. I ran back to my older brother to show him my cool new prize. As I made my way back to our table, I became more and more panicked. I couldn't get my fingers out of the knot. My fingers tugged harder and harder. I tried to use my surrounding fingers to loosen the vice grip on my index fingers. No amount of work on my part was enough to free my fingers. I became so frustrated that I was almost in tears

Anyone who has ever played with a Chinese finger knot understands that the harder you attempt to pull your fingers out of the knot, the tighter the knot becomes. The only way to free yourself is to do the most counterintuitive thing: push your fingers further into the knot. It is only when you lean into the constriction will you finally ease up the tension. When you embrace the stricture, your fingers can finally find freedom.

The same is true with your emotions. Our emotions do not go away. The more we try to escape them, the tighter we bind ourselves. Only instead of getting ourselves stuck in a Chinese knot, we get our minds stuck in a chaos of thoughts. We women are really great thinkers. We are resourceful. We are great problem-solvers. We are also great at thinking about others. In all of this thinking, we are holding ourselves back. We are disconnecting further from our hearts and becoming progressively superficial.

After we become aware of our thoughts, the next step is to embrace the emotions that arise. If thoughts were a window into our unconscious, feelings are the door. Even Ariadne in *Inception* commented that the unconscious is "more about the feel of it" than anything else. But if you're anything like I was, you likely do not know what it means to embrace your emotions or to feel your feelings.

What is a Feeling?

"How do you feel about that?" I asked. (For the record, yes, even I ask the stereotypical shrink question a time or two.)

"Well, I think I'm just so confused right now, I don't really know what to do." I was talking to a patient named Bianca about her stresses around returning to work after the birth of her baby.

"You told me what you're thinking, but what are you feeling?" I probed lightly. While women are usually great at expressing their emotions, they can be horrible at actually embracing their emotions.

"I think—" she stammered.

"I already know what you're *thinking*, what are you *feeling*?" I probed further.

"I think... haha, I mean I feel that I'm letting someone down either way." Whether she stays at home or returns to work, she feels like a failure. Ah, the endless plight of a working mom. I empathize.

"Hmm... you started with "I feel" but you're still telling me a thought," I clarify. This is a common problem. A feeling is one word. A thought is a sentence. If you catch yourself saying a full sentence or an explanation, you are still thinking. You are not feeling.

"Well, I feel... I don't know," she said, disgruntled. She was becoming obviously more frustrated with my line of questioning.

"Okay, let's back up. Forget your thoughts. How would you describe your mood right now?" I reframed to help get to a more positive space.

"I don't know... stressed," she admitted.

"Stressed... good, what other moods would you describe?" I don't let her off the hook that fast. From my experience, "stressed" and "anxious" are ubiquitous to living in America, so I want to get to the bottom of her feelings, the bottom of her heart. Stress and anxiety are merely symptoms of what she's really feeling. And in a bizarre way, I think stress and anxiety have become more appropriate coping mechanisms for patients; therefore, they feel they will be less judged by saying they're stressed or anxious rather than whatever is flowing underneath, which is usually more than one emotion.

"Well, I'm just stressed. I don't know. I'm stressed okay!" she flew up her hands in the air in anger and then let them drop to her lap, letting out a huge sigh.

I waited silently. The silent pause has been challenging for me, but something that has proven therapeutic countless times.

"You don't have anything to say?" she was displacing her emotions onto me, clearly becoming angrier. I can usually tell what a patient is feeling by how she makes me feel when I'm talking to her.

Still silent.

"Ok, I'm angry! I'm angry. I'm angry that I have to leave my son when he's so young. I'm afraid. I'm afraid that I'll miss out on his life. That he'll forget me or something. I don't know. I know it's crazy, but I'm his mother!" she released. I noticed her anger a while back, so hearing her emotion was not news to me.

"Now we're getting there. You're angry and afraid. These are feelings." I smiled proudly at her. Acknowledging the recognition of feelings is incredibly therapeutic.

"Yeah, and I'm sad. I don't want to leave him or abandon him."

It's challenging to look beyond our thoughts and identify our feelings. We learn to suppress our emotions from a young age. Just think of how we raise any child. We usually discipline them when they act out or throw a temper tantrum. Now, I'm not suggesting that we allow our children to overrule us, but I am suggesting that our emotions can be a powerful communication tool when we allow ourselves to experience them.

Why Feelings Are Important

Feelings are communication from the body to the brain. Before we can utter the descriptive word, we experience a sensation in our body. The premier neuroscientist Antonio Damasio is most renowned for his work on somatic (physical) sensations and how they influence our decision-making capabilities. In Damasio's work, he concludes that our somatic sensations, or feelings, are responsible for everything from eating and sex to driving and caring for children. One of his more well-known studies actually showed that without emotional capabilities, beings will starve to death. Meaning, we need emotions to eat. This obviously blows the whole "eat only for fuel" argument out of the water. I digress. From primitive neuroanatomy, our brains are primed to have certain impulses, which are feelings in the body. We don't have words for the impulses because they happen so frequently and with instantaneous speed that more often than not, we do not even recognize their comings and goings.

Like our primitive impulses, our feelings are present to protect us from harm. Over time, we experience countless hurts and heartaches, and all the while, our feelings are there to protect us. In fact, when feelings are powerful enough, they can shut down parts of our memory circuits so that we repress pain and discomfort. Neuroimaging of Posttraumatic Stress Disorder patients show a downregulation of common memory systems when trauma events are activated.[17] It is the reason why it is particularly challenging for PTSD patients to move past their trauma, because many have fully repressed these memories in the first place.

Our brain is divinely created for our benefit. While we cannot see inside of our brain, we can feel our feelings from the body. Yet, if you're like many, you have easily suppressed your feelings for so long. Whether out of sheer survival or deliberation, you have stopped feeling life revolving around you.

When I was in the core of my postpartum depression, I felt as though I was sitting at a train stop. I watched hundreds of trains rushing by me. I was powerless to jump on the train. My legs were glued to the sidelines. All the characters and events of my life were whooshing right in front of my face. And in the brief moments when I raced to get on the train, I couldn't catch up. Even in the midst of my depression, I was so busy judging my depression that I never allowed myself to just be. I hindered my recovery by avoiding my feelings. In order to be you, it's pivotal that you not only recognize your feelings, but you stop judging the feelings that arise.

Feeling Your Feelings

I suffered for almost nine months before I sought treatment for postpartum depression. Although I work in the mental health field, I was somewhat oblivious to the fact that I myself needed help. Like many high-achieving, successful women, I was good at solving my own problems and not making excuses. And I internalized the pervasive stigma that my postpartum depression was a character flaw within my control, rather than a mental illness that could be treated.

When I finally sought treatment, it was only to see a psychiatrist for medication management. While medications were truly life-saving for me, I knew I needed more intensive therapy. The issues that I was facing went beyond issues of new motherhood. Professionally, I see this pattern frequently. Oftentimes, a new mom experiencing postpartum depression is seeking mental health services for the first time. It is likely not the first time she has had issues with mood and anxiety. I was no exception.

Even after being stabilized on medication, I continued to hit wall after wall in quite possibly every segment of my life. After three years, I knew I couldn't avoid therapy any longer. By this time, I was nearing the end of my residency and knew that I would be moving soon. Given that I had limited time and specific goals, I sought a specific kind of therapy that was short-term in nature and specific in scope: Eye Motion Desensitization and Reprocessing Therapy (EMDR).

EMDR therapy was first minted for posttraumatic stress disorder and is still used most traditionally for combat veterans and severe trauma patients, though in recent years it has gained traction in mainstream therapy. Thanks to online marketing expert and fitness trainer, Chalene Johnson, and her bestie, Dr. Mcayla Sarno, EMDR has become vogue in the entrepreneurial circles.

Essentially, EMDR helps to challenge limiting beliefs. Limiting beliefs are beliefs that have infiltrated your core—your heart—and hold us back in life. These beliefs can be things like "I'm not good enough," "I can't do it," or "I'll never succeed." Often, they are so ingrained that they function as an automatic response in certain circumstances, and we don't even consciously realize they're there. Except that they're holding us back. If you have habits in your life that you just can't change, or patterns in relationships that you just can't fix, there is likely some limiting belief holding you back.

Now, there is a right way to do EMDR and a wrong way. You will sit on a couch or chair, facing a monitor or device that has blinking lights that go back and forth in horizontal movements with sounds that help to activate bilateral parts of your brain. I won't go into detail on the exact mechanism, but the research is pretty sound (pun intended). Yet, the biggest mistake I observe is that many patients cannot truly drop down into their hearts to fully *feel* or relive their trauma. When I say "trauma," I mean any situation that causes a heightened sense of emotion. This can be something as small as a fight with your husband, being scolded by your boss, or a stressful outburst from your kids. Any situation that brings up a heightened sense of emotion is likely related to some underlying traumatic experience, oftentimes stemming from childhood.

The whole point of EMDR therapy is that you are essentially reliving your trauma or stressful event and able to process through it. Then, you can face similar situations in the future without the heightened state of emotion. If you are not drenched in tears the first few sessions of EMDR, you're probably not doing it correctly. And I know from experience. The first time I did EMDR, I thought it was totally bogus and that there was no way this works as well as all the research studies show. I was just staring at a flashing light back and forth and giving myself a mild headache in the process.

My therapist looked at me and said, "How do you feel now?"

"Umm, I don't know. Not that much different," I remarked.

"What are you feeling in your body?" my therapist asked.

"Umm, I don't know." Really, I was *that* patient. I was so out of touch with my body that I couldn't even describe a physical sensation.

"Well, let's just focus on what you're thinking," my therapist comforted me. She was so encouraging in those early days.

Yes, yes, thoughts... now, that I can do.

You see, we are so trapped in our thoughts that we literally don't even know what it means to feel. We also get confused about what a feeling is.

It takes practice to feel the emotions rise in your body. You'll notice that emotions tend to come in "waves." You experience the initial crest of the wave. Over the next few moments, the feeling will peak and then crash down and eventually sizzle out, like a wave that calms as it gently rolls up to shore. Feelings, the physical sensations and manifestations in your body, do not last long, sometimes only a few seconds, other times, an entire day. Practice identifying the wave right now.

Describe in words what it feels like to ride the wave. Get specific. Use a dictionary to find synonyms. Instead of happy, maybe you are joyful, abundant, cheerful, or excited. Instead of sad, maybe you are dejected, remorseful, grieving, or empty.

Hearts and Crafts

Draw Your Emotions
· ·

You now have a heart filled with various words, names of people, themes, and possibly some conflicting words or phrases. Now, let's add your emotions.

- ♥ Use crayons or markers to describe your emotions in the colors that you want to demonstrate. Maybe your anger is purple, not red. Maybe your sadness is pink, not blue
- ♥ Add in stickers, textures, patterns, doodles, or graphics to further describe your emotions.
- ♥ If your feeling had a taste, what would it taste like? What is the texture of your feeling? Rough, smooth, crunchy, sticky?
- ♥ Find similarities in nature. Is your feeling like summer, fall, winter, or spring? Are you on top of a mountain or low in a valley?
- ♥ Relate your feelings to activities. Are you swimming in a river or whitewater rafting? Walking on a tight rope or sinking in quicksand?
- ♥ Make note of any competing emotions as well.

Share your heart on Instagram with the hashtag #letyourheartout

Feelings on Top of Feelings

As you begin to acknowledge your feelings, you may notice a few common feelings arise: guilt, shame, embarrassment. These are all common. Yet, these are likely not your pure feeling. I must help you distinguish pure emotions from what I consider secondary or tertiary emotions.

For example, say you are feeling sad when you have to go back to work and leave your baby in daycare. For financial or personal reasons, you must work. Because you do not have a choice, you begin experiencing judgment. Before allowing yourself to feel sadness, you judge yourself. Why did I choose to have a baby at this time? Why didn't I save more money for my maternity leave? Why didn't I plan ahead? What you then experience is guilt for not being a good enough mother.

When you catch yourself experiencing vague feelings or judgmental feelings, look beneath the surface. What else is going on in your life? If you're so inclined, ask yourself: why do I feel as though I cannot express my pure emotion in the first place?

As you begin naming your feelings, it's easy to get caught up in ambiguity.

"How are you feeling today?" I asked one of my long-term therapy patients.

"I don't know... bad." Vi remarked bluntly. Believe it or not, this is not uncommon.

"Okay." I said flatly.

"Haha, I know it's not... what you were expecting," Vi said anxiously. It never ceases to amaze me that we women are so good at pleasing others, even when it comes to sharing your feelings with your therapist.

"What do you mean?" I asked.

"Well, it's just, I don't know, I'm usually doing so well," Vi admitted.

She was right. She normally appeared like she was doing well. But even the best actresses can't hide the pain that comes after a miscarriage.

"Yes, but after your loss, I imagine you would be feeling pretty bad." I reflected. Vi had been having a hard time processing her loss, so I was trying to make a safe space for her to tell me how she really felt.

"I do. Feel bad, I mean. I really do." She burst into tears. The remainder of the 45-minute session was spent sitting. Being still. Allowing Vi to just be in her sadness.

Sitting with your feelings is not be taken lightly. It is one of the most uncomfortable things we can do. It is because of this overwhelming discomfort that we have spent our lives inventing ways to avoid feeling these feelings. I remember the pain I felt when I said goodbye to Travis as he was leaving on deployment to Iraq. It felt as though half my heart was splitting out of my chest and abandoning me. If we can't feel the bad, then we will never appreciate the good. Like in the movie *Inside Out*, we need Sadness in order to feel Joy. The contrasts in life help us appreciate the complex abundance that we live in.

Since we are on the subject of feelings, I must call attention to an important note. While I will always encourage you to feel your feelings fully without judgment, never do I intend your feelings to be the leader of your life. Meaning, feelings let us down. They are subjective, highly personal, and vulnerable to context. We cannot and should not use our feelings to make decisions for us. Feelings deserve their own space in your life, but the goal is not to allow them to consume you.

By feeling your feelings, you will naturally put them in their proper place. It is when we avoid these feelings that they begin to seep into every arena of our lives. To combat this, we must identify our feelings as they arise. If all you can do in the beginning is name your feelings as "good" or "bad," that is okay. Investigating the complexity of your emotions takes time.

Although your feelings are not always reliable indicators of your overall state of being, they are a part of you. Your feelings are not right or wrong, good or bad. They just are. They are you.

As you begin to become aware of your thoughts and emotions, remember to accept the conflict and complexity. For example, when your daughter enters school for the first time, you may be excited for the new milestone but also grieving over the loss of her baby stages. Explore the competing forces at play.

Emotions are as complex as our personalities. Allow the space to feel the breadth of your feelings.

8

*A*nalyze Your Thoughts

"Stefani, what's your superpower?" Kristofer teased with his ninja turtles. At 10 years old, my brother enjoyed taunting 8-year-old me. He and his friend had begun playing war between his ninja turtles and my Barbies. I tried to stay out of the battle, but when he pulled off the heads of one of my Barbies (never to be reaffixed again), I quickly jumped to the rescue.

"I don't know. I don't need a superpower!" I yelled. I was always trying to prove myself to the boys. Admitting I needed a superpower would be ultimate defeat.

"You have to have a superpower!" Kristofer's friend retorted.

"Well, I'm going to fly! Your Barbies can't get me. I'm just going to fly over them." Kristofer taunted, waving his Raphael ninja turtle in my Barbie's face.

My irritation won me over, and I finally conceded, "Fine! My superpower is mindreading! My Barbies will read the minds of your ninja turtles. You won't be able to escape."

Don't ask me why I thought that mindreading in inanimate toys would somehow work, but it was the first idea that popped into my head. As you can imagine, several more Barbies became casualties to that war.

I'm sure my brother doesn't even remember this story. Had it not been for the traumatic association with seeing my Barbie's head get pulled off, I may not remember it either. Funnily enough, my brother is a pilot today, and I am a psychiatrist. While I don't necessarily read minds, sometimes I come pretty close. I guess it's true what they say: you really know yourself best when you're a kid. From a young age, I was fascinated by human behavior and the human brain. I loved people watching, not to judge people but to analyze them and try to figure them out. I imagined what someone was thinking and why they were thinking that. Looking back now, it was only natural that I became a psychiatrist.

In my early days of training, I was enthralled by what I was learning, and I wanted to show off all of my skills to family and friends. Needless to say, not everyone met my "skills" with the same intrigue as I did. I guess there is a reason for informed consent, even in therapy. While I love what I do, I purposefully separate my work from my personal life. Not everyone wants to know themselves better, and it's normal to feel judged or attacked when a professional makes a psychological interpretation of your thoughts or behaviors. Learning to turn off my mindreading powers has served me well in my personal life.

The amount of times I've heard the "don't analyze me" refrain is astounding. I blame pop culture, Freud, and movies like *One Flew Over the Cuckoo's Nest* for society being misinformed about mental health professions. Most people do not know what a psychiatrist does. Truth be told, my husband doesn't fully understand what I do. Even *I* didn't know what a psychiatrist did before becoming one.

I will clarify one thing: traditional psychoanalysis is a separate practice in and of itself. The image of lengthy therapy sessions with a patient lying on a couch and an emotionless therapist taking copious notes and barely uttering a word is the exception to the practice rather than the rule. As I use the word "analyze" throughout this chapter, keep in mind that this pales in comparison to true psychoanalysis from Freud's era. That said, many techniques that I use may overlap with this philosophy. Instead of requiring several hundred hours in therapy, I am empowering you to be your own analyst of your thoughts.

Hearts and Crafts
Analyze Your Thoughts

Review your freestyle. Think about your writing like a storyline. If you're like most of my clients, your writing likely feels rushed and empty. I assure you that even in the most seemingly superficial freestyles there is a story to be told.

♥ What is the overall tone? Angry, sad, rushed, hurried, frustrated? Is there a theme? What topics do you repeat over and over again? Where is the setting? What is the conflict? What are the pain points?

♥ Who is the main character(s)? Are you only writing about yourself or are there other people involved?

♥ Are there any conclusions that you can draw? What underlying message can you glean?

♥ Write conclusions or messages at the bottom of your coloring page.

Share your heart on Instagram with the hashtag #letyourheartout

Find the Association

When a patient of mine, Mia, did the free writing exercise, a majority of her writing was about her clothes and not fitting into her clothes. The word "fit" and the phrases "can't fit," "too tight," and "uncomfortable," arose throughout. Now, it was true that her clothes in that moment did not fit her. She was four months postpartum and still in maternity clothes. This is not an exercise in thought distortions. This is an exercise in the unconscious.

As I was reviewing her writing and speaking to her more, it was abundantly clear that "not fitting in" was an overarching theme in her life at the time. Mia was returning to work and was not only one of the only females in her architecture firm but also the only female with a baby. She did not fit in at work. Also, the environment of her work was very constrictive, and she felt on more than one occasion that she could not fully express her creative side. This was an environment that was "too tight" and "uncomfortable." Furthermore, she was recently left out of a celebration with her in-laws, a common occurrence with that side of her family. This left her feeling dejected, as if she "can't fit" in with her family. She was also in the process of moving, living in cramped quarters with her parents while waiting to move into her new home. This definitely made her feel "uncomfortable." Clearly, the message her heart was trying to communicate was, *I want to fit in. I want to belong. I want comfort.*

An online client of mine, Emmy, repeated the words "want," "different," and "connection" throughout her writing. Mind you, the content of her writing had very little to do with these words, but these particular words were repeated several times throughout. In her life, she was straddling full-time corporate world and a side hustle. She was in the middle of her first book launch. It was also written near the end of the year, so she had naturally been reflecting on her past year. She concluded several different projects at her job and played a new role as breadwinner of her home. Emmy was burned out, frustrated by her job, and felt as though her strengths of connectedness and emotionality were not serving her well in her job. She was exhausted, being pulled in many different directions, and clearly was desiring a change in her life. For her, that meant more connections and less work. The underlying message could be, *I want a different kind of connection* or *I want different connections in my life.*

Lastly, Chelsea, another online client of mine, stressed the importance of "time" and "sleep." At first glance, the context of her writing appeared like a running to-do list. She even joked with me that the majority of her thoughts came in the form of an errand list. Looking a little deeper, she made several references to specific dates and time with regard to her children and her husband. When we put these two themes together, we concluded that she first of all valued time and order in her life. The deeper message though was, *I'm missing out on time with my family* and *I want time for myself.*

These messages may seem contradictory to each other. Wanting time for herself versus feeling like she's missing out on time with her family can seem to be mutually exclusive. But Chelsea's messages bring up an important point to note. While sometimes you may have one clear, coherent message, more often than not you may have two conflicting messages at play.

Confront the Conflicts

You will likely notice that you have several competing desires within you. Your writing may include several questions or thoughts that seem to be contradictory in nature. This is entirely normal. We are constantly pulled from one force to another. It is impossible to ignore the never-ending conflict. Becoming aware of the conflicts will help you understand yourself better and will also provide information to help uncover the real reasons behind your current thoughts and feelings.

My patient, Bianca, had a hard time accepting the fact that she was returning to work after having her son.

"Then, why are you?" I obnoxiously probed. Obviously, I know the answer, and I can understand real-life financial difficulties. I also know that giving space for my patients to talk through their choices out loud helps them to own their decisions instead of feeling like a victim.

"Why am I what?" she replied.

"Leaving him to go back to work?" I reframed to the obvious question at hand.

"Well, because I need the money… and… I love my job," she stammered through the last part. Usually, just hearing your own voice state your concerns can bring to light issues that you didn't know existed.

"Why did you hesitate to say you love your job?" I know I mentioned that I never ask my patients "why." This is true to an extent. As you do become more self-aware, asking why in certain situations is powerful.

"Because, isn't that bad to admit that I love my job? I mean, it's the one thing taking me away from my son, the most important thing in my life right now." She was calming down in front of me. Clearly, she was beginning to make sense of this difficult situation in her life, and the guilt and shame was melting away.

"But you love your job?" I inquired sincerely.

"I do, I really do." Bianca is an asylum attorney, meaning she helps illegal immigrants gain necessary paperwork to remain in the United States safely.

Bianca's story is all-too-common. Working moms have it rough. I speak from experience. Because most jobs in America are not conducive to "bring your kid to work day" every day, we are faced to make a choice. There is a new wave of the #wahm— Work at Home Mom—but many of us professionals and others just do not have the resources or capabilities to transition our career easily to home. Whether by culture, society, or familial expectations, we have an ingrained sense of what is "right" and "wrong." For Bianca, it was wrong to enjoy something that steals away from motherhood. As in, if she didn't want to be with her son 24/7, then she was bad, thus creating the unconscious conflict of two competing ideas. I love my son, but I love my job. Whenever there's a conflict, stress and anxiety are bound to ensue.

To explain further, let me provide an analogy. Imagine riding in a helicopter over a large forest. You spot a smokescreen arising from the treetops. After a quick analysis, you identify a likely forest fire. With this analogy, think of the smoke as your current symptoms: anxiety, fear, depression, stress. Underlying all of these issues is a fire. If you merely try to rid yourself of the smoke, the fire underneath will continue to burn down the forest. The longer you avoid the underlying problem, the more damage it will cause around you. Also, fire is created by two objects in conflict with one another, two sticks rubbing against one another or two rocks increasing friction through beating together. Whichever method you use, it requires conflict, force, and friction to spark a flame. Similarly, the fires below the surface are created from unconscious conflicts.

In my case, I was a working mom who was feeling stressed and depressed. My job was the biggest overarching conflict of my life. Stress and depression were merely the smokescreens. The unconscious conflict for me was, I love having a career, but I also like being home with my baby. Moreover, I felt like I was missing out on my daughter's life. The remedy for me involved communicating with my residency program and adjusting my rotation schedule. I also began communicating my needs to my husband; I sought professional help for my postpartum depression, and I hired help for household chores and part-time babysitting.

Another common example is newlyweds who just moved in together and may be fighting nonstop. The fighting is the smoke. The underlying conflict may be, I love my husband, but I also like to be alone. A good solution to the conflict, rather than fighting, is to provide space to continue living out independent interests or passions, or just to take a break every now and then.

Oftentimes, the solution is not to change some detail of your life, but rather to give yourself some grace through the process. I had very little control of my work schedule in residency. I also didn't have the option to quit without sacrificing literally a lifetime of training. Instead of altering the circumstances of my life, I had to change myself inside.

Know that you will not be all things to all people. Conflict may always exist. Becoming aware of these conflicts is the first step. Accept the conflict for what it is. The goal is not to remove the conflict entirely, but to gain mindfulness around the situation. When you gain deeper awareness, you can begin to associate your current state with potential triggers of your past, thereby understanding more about yourself and why you are the way you are.

Take heart. Reading the examples above may set an unrealistic precedent that analyzing your heart is always straightforward, but that's never the case. It's taken me more than five years of both professional and personal work to define my skill of discernment. Analysis of the heart takes time, reflection, and practice. Give yourself some grace. And once you learn to process the past, you can start to take action toward the future.

9
Reflect on the Past

Anyone who has spent any time around a toddler is familiar with the most common question in the English language: *Why?* Seeking meaning in a given situation is what separates humans from other animal species on the earth. Young children exploring the world naturally ask why. Answering this question helps them gain confidence in an otherwise confusing world.

However, you don't have to be a toddler to ask the question, why? Popular self-development teaches you to start with your why. There's a good reason, too. For instance, if we can understand why we do a certain maladaptive behavior, we have a much higher likelihood of being able to change that unwanted behavior. You may be familiar with the saying, "When you know better, you do better." Knowledge is power.

We also ask why in order to find a deeper purpose. My patients will frequently ask questions such as, "Why me?" "How did this happen to me?" and "What did I do to cause this?" We ask these questions in order to find purpose in our pain. We seek clarity in our suffering. To find purpose and clarity in our heart, we must look past our thoughts, feelings, and analysis of our conscious state. If you remember from earlier, our why is often buried in our unconscious. In order to uncover the why, we need to look to the heartaches of our past.

Dealing with past heartache is not fun. One of my dad's adages is, "Don't live in the rearview mirror." He explains that the rearview mirror was made smaller and out of your eye's line of sight for a reason. What's right in front of you is a much larger, much more important, windshield. Focusing on the rearview mirror will not get you from point A to point B.

In my experience, most women have allowed their rearview mirrors to take the place of their windshields, except they don't even realize it. So, I agree with my dad. Our rearview mirror is much smaller and positioned out of our line's eye for a reason: because it is less important. However, when you have allowed your past to consume your current field of vision, you are crashing your way through life. The goal is to put your rearview mirror back in its proper place in your life. Then, you can regain the clarity and focus you need to avoid accidents and be the safe and competent driver of your life.

Unfortunately, the only way to do that is to process your past. Through processing your past, you come to find the associations between your current thoughts or concerns and your unconscious fears or limitations. These unconscious fears or limitations stem from past hurts, hence the reason we need to investigate our past. Don't worry. You need not process all of your past hurts and struggles. With my technique, we only acknowledge the past if it is interfering with your ability to function in the present.

In this chapter, you will begin to see beyond the surface, to look beyond the superficial and to truly see the core of the matter. Only then can you work through the heart of the issue. To offer some further clarity, let me share an example. I remember a moment two years ago when I had come home from a particularly stressful overnight call shift. I walked into the house and was met with an onslaught of disaster: dishes overfilled the sink, toys were in all rooms of the house, clothes were strewn everywhere. You moms can likely relate. While this scene is not a completely shocking encounter (unfortunately), after a 30-hour call shift while six months pregnant, I was not pleased.

As you can predict, I let out a lot of anger toward my husband. I don't remember the details, but it was likely not pleasant. I was completely fixating on the dishes. The next moment, my husband was holding me in a warm hug and whispering in my hair, "This isn't really about the dishes, is it?" He was right. I was physically exhausted and emotionally drained. I was sad that I missed my weekend of quality time with my family, and tomorrow my husband would drive back to Williamsburg, VA where he was completing his MBA. I was upset about our geographic separation and felt distance in our marriage as a result. And overnight call shifts really suck.

It's never really about the dishes, y'all. Next time you catch yourself bickering about seemingly petty things, remember, you got 99 problems, but the dishes ain't one. Let me guide you to explore what the heart of the matter really is.

Mia's parents got divorced when she was nine years old. After the divorce, she begrudgingly went to live with her mom who had moved out of their childhood home. Mia transferred schools into a new school district. She remembers walking into school and immediately feeling left out. Her fashion was different from girls in her new school, and she was frequently bullied for the clothes that she wore. (It now makes sense why her clothes were the source of her current angst.)

If you're like many of us, these thoughts and feelings began early in our childhood. If you remember Mia's feelings of not feeling like she "fit in," she recalled first feeling like that in her early childhood.

Mia had recently moved across the country for her husband's job. This cross-country move separated her from her close friends and family from back home. As already mentioned, she felt as though she didn't fit in to her current life.

Hearts and Crafts

Reflect on the Past

Review your coloring page thus far.

- ♥ Recall the first time that you remember feeling this way in your life.
- ♥ Describe that time in your life with as much detail as possible.
- ♥ Find the association in the present. What about your current reality is similar to that particular time in your life?
- ♥ Write your reflections on your coloring page.

Share your heart on Instagram with the hashtag #letyourheartout

As you make associations between the here and now and your past, you may realize that you still harbor pain from baggage in your past. We all have baggage, so you are not unique in this struggle. No one escapes childhood unscathed. What differentiates the self-aware from the self-destructive are those who are determined to let go of their baggage.

Stop Carrying Around Your Baggage

I remember taking our first trip with two children. We were traveling to Texas for the holidays to visit my parents and my in-laws. If traveling with one child was a challenge, traveling with two kids was a circus. (My heart goes out to you mamas with more than two kids. Can't. Even. Imagine.) Not to mention, we were running late for our flight. (Thanks, D.C. traffic.) While I was carrying a squirming six-month-old Ryker in the Ergobaby and managing an impatient 3-year-old Kate, Travis was bravely coordinating our seemingly infinite amount of baggage. He positioned our two car seats, stroller, and large suitcase on a dolly while slinging a duffel bag on one shoulder, two diaper bags on the other shoulder, and a large backpack on his back. It was a sight.

Making an early morning flight was sleep-depriving enough, but juggling several pieces of luggage with two cranky, young children left us drained. By the time we maneuvered from parking garage to baggage claim, we were exhausted. However, the weight of releasing the baggage was freeing. Being able to walk nearly empty-handed through security and onto the airplane was gratifying. Even if we manage to unload our baggage from time to time, it still flies with us on our journey of life. Eventually though, we need to unpack our bags altogether.

Unpack Your Baggage

If there's one thing worse than traveling with luggage, it's unpacking your bags. After I return from vacation or travel, I will take several weeks to unpack my bags. No joke. I once waited two months before unpacking my bags. I was practically living out of my suitcase. And at the time of this writing, there is still an unpacked piece of luggage of my husband's lying on our bedroom floor from a trip he took two weeks ago. He is traveling again tomorrow, but that's beside the point. For sake of analogy, go with me.

Why is it so painful to unpack our bags? We may be afraid of what we will see in there. (With small kids, you never know.)

Though, more likely, we know exactly what is in there. That is precisely the reason why we avoid it. We don't want to unpack our bags. We want to stay on vacation where we can avoid the pain and hurt of our reality. We are comfortable in the realm of fantasyland. We are professional escape artists. Avoidance has become our mantra. Don't believe me? Revisit earlier chapters.

It's not that we are afraid of the unknown. We are more afraid of what we *do* know. We assume that if we don't unpack our bags, then life isn't happening. I hate unpacking my bags. I talk to many women, and this is a fairly common problem. Most people do not like unpacking their bags. It's annoying, frustrating, and time-consuming. Maybe what is the least fun of all is the finality. Once I unpack my bags, I'm no longer on vacation. That means I'm back to real life, with all the pressures, stressors, and trials that come with real life. Vacation illustrates escape for us. While it's not always bad or wrong to escape once in a while, the majority of us are living our lives in constant escape-mode. Always avoiding what is real and true, and striving for some fictional state of being has become our drug of choice. To stop avoiding, we must start processing the hurt head on.

Process the Hurt

Nearing the end of my intern year of my psychiatry residency, I was rotating on our inpatient psychiatric unit. It was a particularly challenging day, as one of the attending psychiatrists was out, so I was receiving phone calls regarding 20 patients on the unit as well as incoming admissions from the emergency department. I also had a one-year-old at home and she had recently decided she didn't want to sleep through the night. I was exhausted. Drained. Burned out. Compassion fatigued. I had it all. I was ready for intern year to be done already.

"Hey Stefani, let's do a CSV," my attending demanded. Where did he come from? I hadn't even seen him on the unit until now. A Clinical Skills Evaluation (CSV) is required for all psychiatry residents. Basically, your attending watches you do a structured, comprehensive patient interview. Then, you present your biopsychosocial assessment and plan for the patient. After, you receive feedback from your overseer. You either pass or fail, and you have to pass three before you graduate residency.

"Umm, now?" I asked apprehensively. *He must have felt the nervousness and exhaustion in my voice,* I thought to myself. This attending was particularly known to fail most interns. I already had hours of work ahead of me. Not to mention I had never even done a CSV before.

"Yeah, let's go," he said matter-of-factly as he walked to his office, barely giving me eye contact. He clearly missed my oh-so-obvious reservations.

As expected, he did fail me. Not only that, but the patient I interviewed was verbally aggressive and threatening; he had completely thrown off any presupposed ability of me being poised and thorough in a patient interview. I got emotional listening to feedback from my attending. I felt on the brink of tears. He was criticizing everything about my interview style, though I internalized most of it as an attack on me as a person.

At the end of this hour-long ordeal, I retreated to our call room where I found an upper-level resident. Fatima was just about the kindest, most articulate resident. She was a great teacher, easy to work with, and didn't make you feel like a grunt. She also had this calming presence when you were around her, so calming in fact that I broke down in tears right in front of her.

"Oh no, what happened?" she patiently nudged. This was not the first time that this particular attending made an intern cry. Fatima had heard countless stories from other interns and residents.

"I did my first CSV, and it was awful," I blubbered. Fatima came and gave me a hug. I proceeded to tell her my grand plans of transferring residencies. (Escape artist here. Guilty as charged.)

"No, no, no…" she comforted. "You need to process this and move on." She proceeded to listen as I emotionally vomited on her. Clearly, I had been escaping a lot of emotions that year.

We throw around the word "processing" a lot in psychiatry, so I knew a little about what it meant, though it's not uncommon to be clueless when it comes to "processing." I'll break it down for you in plain English. It means thinking through a situation fully, coming to more logical conclusions, feeling whatever emotions arise in that moment, and then letting it go.

How did I process this particular incident? I asked myself… why was I so emotional at that moment? *Well, I didn't sleep well last night, I was working 60+ hours each week with some overnight shifts, I didn't really enjoy what I was doing, and I had failed. I also internalized criticism of my professional abilities as criticism of my sense of self.* Then, I excused myself to the bathroom and cried. (I cried a lot in the bathroom my intern year. #noshame)

I wasn't able to go much deeper than my thoughts and emotions at the time, but since then, I now know that because he was criticizing my performance, it brought forth certain childhood beliefs of inadequacy and unworthiness. For many years of my life, I intertwined my external achievements with my internal worthiness. This pattern is an oh-so-common problem for many high achieving perfectionists.

Repetition Is Not the Key to Learning

My cardiology class in medical school was taught by a popular professor who lived by the mantra "repetition is the key to learning." He repeated this phrase so many times that we almost had fundraising shirts made for him. When one of my classmates played the role of this professor in a roast, we immediately recognized the signature phrase.

While repetition may be the key to learning anatomy and physiology in medical school, repetition is often a destructive compulsion in matters of the heart. As we become more familiar with identifying the heart of the issue, we may observe similar patterns at play. We internalize certain thoughts, behaviors, and interrelationship dynamics at a young age. Through watching how others around us act, and respond and relate to one another, we become conditioned to continue the legacy. This repetition compulsion, as it is called in psychodynamic therapy world, explains why certain maladaptive coping skills— like dysfunctional relationships, bad tempers, eating disorders and substance use—tend to run in families.

However, the repetitive behaviors are not usually as dramatic as addiction, trauma, and severe dysfunction. More commonly, we take on the same habits, behaviors, and communication style as trusted role models in our life, and we oppose the standards of those who have hurt or harmed us. If your husband has ever compared you to your mother, then you know what I'm talking about. At times, I still catch myself reacting to my husband in the same manner that my mom reacted to my dad. Even though I consciously wish to change my behaviors, I must understand the unconscious limitations before I can change the unwanted behavior. It is not enough to be aware of the repetitive behaviors and maladaptive coping skills. We must understand *why* we are engaging in the repetition compulsion in the first place. To define the why, we must become aware of our limiting beliefs.

Limiting Beliefs

If you have seen the movie *Inside Out*, you may be familiar with the vocabulary of core memories. In the movie, core memories were memories that held integral characteristics of the main character, Riley. When the core memories were tainted, Riley's overall demeanor, behaviors, and actions changed. Similarly, our core beliefs are unconscious beliefs that we form based on memories, events, or interactions from a very young age.

These are developmental patterns that we come to associate with our sense of self. Unfortunately, we do so at a level unbeknownst to our conscious awareness. Thus, not all core beliefs we form are helpful, which is why we continue to repeat similar behaviors of those from our childhood.

Limiting beliefs are those core beliefs that do exactly as their name implies. They limit us, hold us back, and prevent us from seeing ourselves and living our lives fully from the heart. If you followed the exercises in the previous chapters, you have gained all the awareness needed to now take one step deeper: acknowledging your limiting beliefs.

If you have a difficult time changing bad habits or you engage in the same dysfunctional relationship patterns, you likely have internalized limiting beliefs in your life. Addictive behaviors, poor coping skills, or irrational expression of emotions can all stem from limiting beliefs.

We develop these limiting beliefs and habitual patterns early in childhood. We then usually continue to play out these similar scenes with different people in our lives. Your current emotions then have very little to do with your current situation and much more to do with people from your past. For instance, maybe the current situation with your husband reminds you of how your dad made you feel growing up. And maybe you express these same emotions when your kids do not pick up their toys, you get jerked around by your boss, or your friend cancels plans at the last minute. Identifying the limiting beliefs that are holding you back is not to place blame, but rather to develop empowering beliefs.

Hearts and Crafts
Limiting Beliefs
. . . .
Review your heart from the previous chapters.

- ♥ In what situations have you reacted this way in the past? What do these situations have in common?
- ♥ Envision the first time in your life when you began feeling this way.
- ♥ Identify the limiting belief.
- ♥ Reframe the limiting belief into an empowering phrase that resonates most with you.
- ♥ Write the empowering belief at the top of your coloring page.

Share your heart on Instagram with the hashtag #letyourheartout

Limiting beliefs swim under the surface of the issues at hand. It requires some introspection to find out what is really going on. In the case of Mia, a limiting belief may be, "I never fit in." For Emmy, the limiting belief could be, "I can't connect with others." In Chelsea's scenario, a limiting belief may be, "There's never enough time."

Other common examples that arise are, "No on loves me," "I'm not good enough," "I can't do this," and "I'm all alone." Or it could be some variant of these.

Once you recognize the deeper source of your limitation, you can begin to insert new empowering beliefs, such as "I am good enough," "I can do this," or "I am valuable." This takes time and practice to recognize these patterns. And it will continue to evolve over time as well, so be patient with yourself.

10
Take Action

I used to live my life by the motto "act first, think later." I'm naturally a bold, outgoing person who finds taking action fairly easy. That said, taking action without substance will only lead to endless frustration. If you remember from Chapter 3, I mentioned that doing more is likely the primary catalyst for the problems in your life. However, if you have followed the steps in the previous chapters, you now have the self-awareness to act with intention. Taking action becomes the easy part.

For Mia, we brainstormed ways in which she could feel like she "fit in." In order to help feed this desire of belonging, we talked about environments where she did fit in. At the time, she fit in with her closest girlfriends and church prayer group. She then made a plan to spend time with those people within the next week.

Emmy was wanting to have different connections in her life. As she was launching her book, she found ways to stick to more one-on-one interviews and less corporate speeches. She found connectedness in sharing her story with individuals rather than large audiences.

Chelsea made a schedule to reallocate her time better. She scheduled time to pamper herself, and she made arrangements to spend uninterrupted time with each of her children over the next week. By giving herself time and space that she needed, she felt rejuvenated. Quality time with her children made her feel full.

Chelsea also made an effort to keep record of special memories of her children. She wanted to feel as though time was not slipping her by, so she began journaling and taking more pictures of her kids. This gave her the illusion that time had slowed down.

Sometimes we cannot give ourselves exactly what we need in that moment. We can at least find some action that brings us the feeling that we want to feel. For Mia, she wanted to feel connected to others. Beyond feeling connected to a specific social group, she acknowledged that cuddling her baby and spending time with her husband also brought the feeling of belonging that she craved.

Hearts and Crafts
Take Action

. . . .

Review your freestyle and your coloring page. What messages did you uncover?

♥ Find immediate ways to fulfill your heart. Write down actions that you can take on your coloring page outside of your heart. The actions you take are a by-product of your heart, not your heart exclusively.

♥ Seek out ways to reenact the feeling that you want to feel. Record different ways you can reenact your feelings on your coloring page.

Share your heart on Instagram with the hashtag #letyourheartout

When I was going through postpartum depression, my job was the biggest source of stress. I had very little control over my work hours though. Since I had such little control in my work life, I craved some control in my personal life. One of the only things I did have control over was my hairstyle. I treated myself to a stylish new haircut and new highlights. It helped me feel better inside when I at least could control one part of myself, if only just a hairstyle.

If you'll indulge me for a moment, let's stop to reflect on how different this process is from traditional self-development out there. Had Mia sought traditional self-development, she would have shared her number one problem, being not fitting into her clothes. After doing a little bit of analysis, she was instead able to see that the real problem was her desire to belong. No amount of diet or exercise would have fed Mia's true desire.

Had Emmy gone after a large vision of changing the world, she would've easily become frustrated with a lack of clarity and wouldn't have known how to take the next step. If Chelsea had tried to increase her productivity and improve time management, she may have gotten more done but wouldn't have uncovered the real issue, which was wanting to spend more time for herself and with her kids. Then, she would've become trapped in the treacherous do-more-feel-less cycle.

When you become aware of the real problems, it becomes fairly straightforward to find a solution that will actually help you feel better and achieve real change that you crave. Believe it or not, though, not all introspection requires action at the end.

Change Your Thoughts

Maybe you realize that instead of taking action with your feet, you need to take action with your mind in the form of changing your thoughts. If you recall, 98% of your approximate 60,000 thoughts per day are on a repetitive loop. When you cannot HEAR what is underneath the thoughts, the right action for you to take may be to correct the thoughts.

At the most basic level, we need to become aware of our current thought distortions. Thought distortions are based in a therapy style known as cognitive behavioral therapy. In cognitive behavioral therapy (CBT), cognitive distortions stem from suppressed, unpleasant emotions and lead to unwanted behaviors to cope. Unwanted behaviors can be as benign as nagging your husband or yelling at your kids, or they can be more destructive, like addictions, drugs, or alcohol. For purposes of the HEART framework, correcting these cognitive distortions may be vital to complete your work.

Hearts and Crafts
Thought Distortions
. . . .

To put this into practice, think of a recent instance that brought you discomfort or stress.

- What is the first thought that comes to mind?
- Challenge the validity of the thought. Is this thought true? As in, can it be held up in the court of law?
- Rewrite a thought explaining the situation that is true.

Share your heart on Instagram with the hashtag #letyourheartout

An example of a distressing situation could be something simple, like being cut off in traffic, or something big, like getting in a fight with your husband, or something common, like your four-year-old not picking up her toys (just me?). Here's an example of challenging your thought distortions:

Concerning the situation of my four-year-old not picking up her toys, my initial thought may be: *My daughter never listens to me.* Then, I challenge the validity of the thought, which is false. My daughter does listen to me sometimes. Last, I reframe the situation to a statement of truth. Instead of, *'My daughter never listens to me,'* I could say, *'My daughter is whining.'*

It is not important that you name the specific kind of distortion that you are using. To help you gain more awareness, though, I will include most common ones here so you can start identifying distorted thoughts (note that this list is not exhaustive).

- ♥ *Polar thinking*: all-or-nothing, black-and-white thinking; putting everything in reference to extremes.
- ♥ *Filtering*: extracting the negative from the positive and focusing only on the negative of a situation without understanding the situation as a whole.
- ♥ *Overgeneralizing*: generalizing an entirety of a situation or person based on one specific entity.
- ♥ *Mind-reading*: assuming you know what someone is thinking or feeling based on your own judgment without facts to back it up.
- ♥ *Fortune-telling*: predicting the future based on current situations.
- ♥ *Catastrophizing*: blowing a situation out of proportion to the event.
- ♥ *Personalization*: making a situation entirely about you, whether through causing a situation or centering details around yourself.

- ♥ *Fallacy of Fairness*: assuming how things should be based on false pretenses of fairness.
- ♥ *Shoulds*: feeling pressure of external circumstances to act or be a certain way.
- ♥ *Blaming*: placing responsibility on someone or something outside of your control.
- ♥ *Emotional Reasoning*: believing something is true because of the way it feels.
- ♥ *Heaven's Reward Fallacy*: expecting rewards for current or past trials and unpleasant events.

It stands to reason that the majority of thoughts we have in a day are based on lies or distortions. Correcting these patterns does take conscious effort for a period of time. As you begin to challenge your thinking, it becomes much easier with practice. Over time, you do not stop distorted thinking altogether, but the act of correcting your thoughts becomes second nature. You recognize your whirling spirals of lies before it causes self-destruction. You then can quickly maneuver your way out of the muddy swamp of thoughts into the land of peace and truth, the land of the real you.

For extra help challenging your thoughts, sign up for my free video series at www.attackanxietynow.com.

When the Right Action Is No Action

"Stefani, what're you doing?" Maddy, my medical school roommate, slowly cracked the door to my bedroom opened.

"Uh, I'm painting?" I said sheepishly. *Omg, this is so embarrassing. This looks horrible, why did she have to walk in on me like this?*

"Umm, are you okay?"

"Yeah, I'm good." *No, I'm not. I'm stressed out of my mind. We're in the middle of exam week, don't you realize that?* I quickly

112

reached for my glass of wine and took a swig so that I didn't have to go into this with her.

"Okayyy…" She lingered. Her perplexed expression and her tone of voice spoke volumes.

I didn't know what to say. I literally had no words. I didn't know why I was painting a wall in my bedroom. Obviously, it was the absolute last thing I needed to be doing in that moment. I needed to pull my grades up in pathophysiology class. I really should have been more focused on my studies.

"Really, Maddy, I'm fine. I just… wanted… a change." *Yeah, that's it. I want a change.* She has to buy that. Hopefully, she'll just leave me be.

She gave me one last inquisitive look before turning on her heel and leaving my room.

I looked back at my shoddy paint job. This was the worst. Not only had the color of paint let me down when I saw it on my walls, but I had run out of the original color. When I returned to the store to get the same color, they mixed the paint improperly (or I gave them the wrong color swatch). I tried to make some sponge paint deco on the wall. Instead, it looked like a preschooler's art project. On my wall. In my apartment. My rented apartment.

I knew I had to paint this back, but now I would have to tell the apartment complex what I had done. Who knows what they will do when they find out? I've heard horror stories of friends getting charges for destruction of property when they did similar things in this apartment complex. By the looks of my less-than-stellar paint job, destruction of property seemed about right. I was so screwed.

All the while, I was wasting precious hours of the day dwelling about the color of my wall and not studying for my classes. (Which, by the way, was the heart of the issue. I was avoiding the ugly stress of my exams by trying to make something pretty in my life, my wall). I needed to put the paint brush down and walk away. Clearly, the more I acted to improve this wall, the worse my situation was becoming.

There are times in life when taking action may actually hurt or harm you, or at least ruin your walls. In these moments, you'll notice that the actions you will be taking have less to do with new behaviors and more to do with continuing to process the chaos inside of your mind. We are conditioned to act. Our society reinforces taking big action. We erroneously assume that making big change in our lives requires some profound action step. It's just not the case. The biggest work of all is the work in your mind.

If you have confusion over any part of the previous chapters, you are not ready to take action. Believe me. Wait for the clarity to come. Take some time to review your work in the previous chapters. Share your work with a trusted friend, lover, family member, or professional. See if they can offer you insights that you may be missing. If you want a little more help, I'd love to work with you individually. Please visit letyourheartoutbook. com for more information on how to work with me directly.

Putting HEART in Practice

I grew up in a football family in Texas. Both of my brothers played football and my dad is now a high school football coach. The intensity of Texas high school football practices is unmatched. My brothers would practice two-a-days in 100-degree weather, months before practice began. There was no such thing as offseason. Spring training was taken as seriously as in-season practice.

When I was growing up, I thought my brothers spent every single day of the week practicing on the football field. What I didn't realize is half of the practice was not spent on the field but was either spent on sports conditioning in the weight room or watching game film. Before they ever set foot on the football field for a practice, let alone a real game, they had spent twice as many hours in the weight room or game film room. Some of the best professional football players to date spend hours reviewing game film, analyzing their opponents, and reflecting on their own pain points. We never see this work, but you can tell the good players from the excellent players by how much they have studied for the game.

You have now reviewed the game film in your mind. You have done extensive work getting to the root of the issues at hand. Now that you understand the HEART framework, it is time to get it out of your head and into your daily life. Just as a professional football player needs to put his knowledge into practice before stepping out on the playing field, you need to use all of the knowledge that you have surmised into your life.

Furthermore, some of you may need to see the HEART in action before you can fully understand the exercises from previous chapters. If you noticed that nothing came to the surface as you engaged in the Hearts and Crafts exercises, you will be comforted to read the next part where I walk you through the HEART in your everyday life.

Keep in mind that your thoughts are unconscious for a reason: to protect you. This is why I initially recommended you do this exercise in an environment where you feel most comfortable. If you were feeling reserved or unsafe doing the exercise, you were likely defending yourself from the most painful parts and hindering your ability to uncover your heart. Give it time. As with any new hobby or skill, comfort and familiarity take practice. Practice finding the heart.

PART 3

Find Your Heart

Heartstrings bind us
Like a puppet, we go
To and fro, we move
For everything and everyone
Outside of us, we don't know
How to remove these ties
So tight, we can't move
Can't breathe, Losing steam
The knots, they quench us
Until we fight no more, we fight
To release the ties
That bind us no more

-Stefani Reinold

11
Beyond the Rulebook

If you've seen the ABC television show, *Once Upon a Time*, you're familiar with the Evil Queen Regina. In the beginning, she is pure evil, cursed to darkness and, as such, torments those around her. She steals hearts in order to imprison people; while she holds the keys to their hearts, she has power and control over them, and if they step out of line, she can inflict physical pain or brainwash them. (In case you're wondering, this show is not kid-friendly.) In one episode, Regina's Huntsman challenges her authority. To put him back in his place, she retreats to her dungeon and retrieves a locked box containing the Huntsman's heart. She proceeds to squeeze his heart in her grip, suffocating and nearly killing him.

When I think of that image, I see many women. I see my friends. I see my colleagues. I see myself. Except instead of having an Evil Queen squeezing our heart, we have done the restricting ourselves. We have allowed the evil forces around us and the darkness within to consume our power, our greatness, our beauty. We have settled into the pain of perpetual tightness and constriction to the point that we cannot even breathe. We must breathe in order to do this work. In order to breathe, we must first remove the ties that bind us.

Rules

Before I met my husband, I read lots of dating books. I was lame, I know. But I'm pretty good at getting what I want: I research it, plan for it, and then, poof, it happens! Of course, it doesn't always happen the way I planned. Actually, rarely do things turn out as planned.

Nonetheless, it assuaged my anxiety to have steps to follow. It provided the alluring sense of control that we're all so freaking desperate for. When I was sick of being single and getting my heart crushed by pathetic boys, I wanted the guidebook for "finding your husband." What did I do? I bought a book. A few books actually. *Love in 90 Days* by Dr. Diana Kirschner was the one book I read from start to finish. In fact, I loved it so much that after I met my now husband, I pawned it off to a fellow hopeless romantic. There are many things I like about the book. At the time, I credited it for my success in finding my husband. When I look back, though, it wasn't the book that helped; it was my own peace of mind.

One of the tenets of the book is to take the stress out of dating. My apologies in advance if I butcher these principles. I don't own the book anymore, so I'm paraphrasing here. I do remember that she recommends dating two to three people at once. At first glance, that may sound kind of naughty for you fellow good girls. I grew up in a conservative Christian home under the notion that dating was an avenue for marriage. The idea of casual dating or fun buddies was not really my jam. Nonetheless, I took her heed and started meeting people. I signed up for a few online dating profiles and began mingling with more men in my immediate social circles. Sure enough, I found love in 90 days.

It was not about meeting as many people as possible and slowly weeding out the bad eggs to find the hidden gem (although I think that is kind of what she talks about in the book). What I found, though, was that for the first time in my dating life, I took the pressure off the situation. I wasn't going into each date with the mindset of "will I marry this man?" and all the heat that adds to the dating encounters. Whether you say it or not, men can feel this kind of energy and most men are turned off by this kind of pressure. No one wants to feel as though they're constantly being seen as a piece of meat, and that's exactly what you do when you're eyeing your prey up and down for "marriage" material from date number one.

Back to my point. When I took the pressure off of each encounter, I began to relax into myself. I started to drop down to what I really wanted. Researchers and gurus refer to this as the abundance mentality. When you're viewing each and every encounter with a guy as if he could be "the One," you are in scarcity mindset. Because what happens if this guy isn't the one or it doesn't work out? You've failed yet again and you're alone. Yet, if you are dating two to three people at once, you get a lot of free dinners. (When you're living on student loans in med school, you take what you can get.) Beyond free dinners, dating multiple people brings out the air of abundance. I can say to myself "Hey, if it doesn't work out with Joe, at least I'm going out with Bob tomorrow."

Sure, I still dreamed of the idyllic, storybook, love-at-first-sight kind of first date, but I broadened my comfort zone. I no longer was holding onto the belief that there is a "right" way to meet someone. In fact, I met my husband through an online dating site and our first date was actually my third date that week. Before you go thinking crazy things, I assure you that after my first date with Travis (my now husband), I stopped dating anyone else. I guess it's true what they say: when you know, you know.

While I may have met my husband after reading a playbook, I don't credit the success of my relationship to the rules. Like I said, nothing ever turns out as planned anyway. And rules are a veil to our underlying fears. We like rules, following them, and creating them. It's why counting calories, or following a fool-proof system to finding love, or buying online courses are so enticing. We want to know the steps. If I do X, Y, and Z, then I'll have the ideal body. If I do X, Y, and Z, then I'll have a successful business. But what then? Not only is your logic flawed, not everyone who does follow all the rules imposed on them will attain wealth or an ideal body or love. *Love in 90 Days* was sadly not the first book I ever read in an effort to win over a man. Travis just happened to be the first guy I met who was my right man. When rules do work out, though, the rush is addicting. We are fed the notion that if this went to plan, then other things in my life can go just like this.

Now, I'm not advocating that you stop following all rules. There is a divine reason we have certain systems in place. Laws and rules ensure our safety and protect our freedom. That's not what I'm talking about. I'm talking about the self-inflicted rules that torment our brains whether anyone is keeping up with us or not.

Standards

Knock. Knock. Knock. "Hello, anyone in here?" as I hear the sound of a key turn on the other end.

Panicked, I grabbed the doorknob. Somehow, I've forgotten to speak. *Do I say something? They'll recognize my voice. What will they think?* Lost in my thoughts, the knob starts turning against my grip. They're going to enter unless I say something.

"Yes", I mumble, "YES…" more confidently, "Yes, I'm in here." *Do they even know who I am? Oh well, the knocker left.*

I'm sitting in the inpatient psychiatric unit bathroom with all of my pumping equipment attached to me. I began my intern year with an eight-week-old, and, only four months postpartum, I'm still determined to keep breastfeeding her. Because? Because... everyone says that you breastfeed for at least six months. The good moms? They breastfeed until baby stops nursing, but at least a year and some up to two years. Oh goodness, I was feeling sick to my stomach. Would I have to keep pumping in cleaning closets and bathrooms until my daughter was two years old?

If you haven't seen an inpatient psychiatric unit before or you've never been privy to its bathrooms, let me paint a picture for you. First of all, everything is locked. The unit is locked. The bathrooms are locked. Some treatment rooms are locked. All of the staff has the keys. When you're trying to use a locked staff bathroom on the same floor just a few feet away from a psychotic patient, it's (a) not the most tranquil experience imaginable for pumping and (b) not the most private place given that any staff could use their key to open the door at any moment. Not to mention the strange looks you get from staff and patients alike after being in the bathroom for 20 minutes at a time, three times a day.

Before you go thinking my residency program sucks for not supporting mothers returning to the workforce, I accept this blame as my own. I didn't speak up. I felt powerless. We could go into a whole slew of reasons why I didn't feel I had a say, but anyone who's been a medical intern before or any low-status, oppressed position can definitely understand. There are some times in life that you just don't think you have any say. And if you literally could speak up (I mean, I do have a functioning voice box here), you know that nothing would really change the situation. Worse, some harm could come to you.

Needless to say, I didn't continue pumping much longer. And slowly, my milk dried up and I could no longer breastfeed my baby. Truth be told, she actually stopped nursing before my milk totally dried up. I'm sure the lactation consultants would say it's because I worked so many hours that she was more comfortable with a bottle, so eventually she lost interest in nursing. And they would likely also say to just "fight through it," that "all babies go through a boob rejection phase," and whatever other BS they tell you.

Look, this isn't meant to be a slight against lactation consultants. Obviously, they do good work for women who need and want the help. But it's my experience that before you subscribe anything to new moms, you need to look at the whole mother. And if breastfeeding appears to be causing more harm than good in this particular mother at this particular moment, then perhaps breastfeeding is just not right for her. And that's ok.

Ladies, especially you fellow moms, think about what ridiculous habits, behaviors, rules, guidelines, or standards you are inflicting on yourself right now. In case you're oblivious to the standards that may be holding you back, here are some common examples that ruffle women:

- ♥ Breastfeeding when it is causing you more harm than good.
- ♥ Feeding your child in general.
- ♥ Staying at home when you wish you were working.
- ♥ Working when you wish you were staying at home.
- ♥ Having sex because you are afraid of hurting your husband's feelings.
- ♥ Faking an orgasm.
- ♥ Dieting, tracking calories, fasting, clean eating, and any other disordered eating.
- ♥ Meticulously nitpicking your body and obsessing with weight loss.
- ♥ Interior decorating because of a Pinterest post.
- ♥ Working out in ways that do not bring you joy.
- ♥ Posting on social media about a "highlight reel" moment because you want attention.
- ♥ Starting a side hustle because you feel you should, not because your heart is in it.

- ♥ Holding impeccable cleanliness standards.
- ♥ Cooking when you don't enjoy it.
- ♥ Not communicating your needs and denying your true desires.

This is not an exhaustive list by any measure, but it gives you an indication where you may be suffering. You probably have a lot to tell me about this list too. Well, doesn't every woman fake an orgasm a time or two? Doesn't everyone suppress their needs for the sake of those around them? And what if I do like putting on a good front to the world? Is there something wrong with that?

Answer me this, are you engaging in these practices from your heart? Most likely, the answer is no. I'm just throwing that out there. Likely, this is from years, decades even, of living for someone or something outside of yourself. Let me ask you one thing: how's that working out for you? How do you really feel living up to (or more commonly, failing to live up to) the external pressures around you? Is anyone driving you to do this, except you? Really, would your husband leave you if you denied sex when you didn't feel like it? Would your health actually be affected if you stopped dieting? (Well, actually, it would improve, but that's for another day.)

How much of your life is spent doing things that are not from the heart? Associating with people who don't bring you joy? Interacting in ways that are not you? If you're like most of us, a helluva lot of the time. You're not alone. Don't get me wrong. I'm not claiming that life should be this *Sound of Music* singing from the hills kind of joy, day in and day out. We will do some things we don't feel like doing every once in a while and will be forced into positions where we just have to survive. I'm only asking you to challenge your motives, because if the majority of your life is spent living for outside standards, you will never enjoy the pure bliss that comes from living from the heart.

If you won't do it for yourself, do it for those around you. There is nothing more irritating than being around a Superficial Sally. You know the ones. (Heck, we've all been the ones.) They appear pretty from the outside, doing the right things, saying the sweet words, but all you feel when you're around them is emptiness. Why? Because they're not living from their hearts. They've lost touch with who they really are. Now all you see is the translucent shell on the outside. We don't see her unique presence, spiritual gifts, or eclectic beauty. All we see from them is the world around them mirroring back to their souls.

A Last Note on Guilt

Guilt is pervasive these days. It's even become a popular hashtag: #momguilt. While I've been guilty of using the hashtag (pun intended), we have to challenge this. Guilt is not a feeling, slang, or some cool new trend. Guilt is the direct result of self-inflicted misery brought on by not living up to an ambiguous external policy, rule, or standard. Period. End of story.

Guilt never comes from the heart. It does not arise from a good place, and it never catapults you further in life. It weighs you down, not to the bottom of your heart, but to the bottom of your misery. Guilt creates a barrier between you and others in your life, prevents you from growing spiritually, and hinders the boundaries you hold so dear. Guilt is only a symptom of some deep emotion tied up with an external influence. When you challenge the outside pressures of your life, you release the confines of guilt in a flash.

Find Your *HEART*

- 💜 **Here and Now.** What rules or self-imposed standards are you following right now?
- 💜 **Embrace Your Emotions.** How does it make you feel when you imagine breaking these rules?
- 💜 **Analyze Your Thoughts.** What could your thoughts and feelings about following these rules be communicating to you about your life as a whole?
- 💜 **Reflect On Your Past.** When do you first remember feeling this way in the past?
- 💜 **Take Action.** Break the rules. Choose one rule that you have been following obediently and make a plan to purposefully break the rule. Within the confines of the law, of course.

12
More than Sex and Romance

"I want to get you something," Travis said. We were sitting in his truck. We had played golf together that morning and had just finished lunch at Cheddar's.

"Okay," I said flatly. I was never going to turn down a sweet gift from my boyfriend.

"Okay?" Travis smirked. He always answers statements with questions and questions with questions. He's a pro at asking questions.

"Okay." I smiled. He leaned over and kissed me softly. His sweet tongue entwined with mine. I could still taste the ice cream in his breath. I was going to miss this. We had been dating for the past eight months. I loved him. He loved me. It was that all-consuming bliss only found in the beginning of a new Love.

"How about we go in and you pick something out?" He was already getting out of the car. He came around to my side and opened the door for me to get out. But first he met his lips to mine once more. This time, quick and swift, like a habit. He still kisses me when we get in the car. I like this habit.

"Sounds like a plan." There was no special occasion to celebrate, unless you considered him leaving on deployment in one week a special occasion. I'm sure he could tell I was not handling it well. I had already cried a few times in the past week.

I felt the warmth as he placed his hand on the small of my back and walked into James Avery to look around. His touch warmed my soul. He had become my best friend. Moreover, he was one of my only real friends. And my boyfriend. And my love.

We proceeded to look around. "Why don't you look at the rings?" he suggested, as he led me to the front of the store where the rings were displayed.

After trying on a few rings, I picked out a classic pearl ring. Travis paid out with the cashier. When I tried to grab at the bag, he quickly said, "Just wait until we get back to the car."

Confused, I followed him back to the car. He helped me into his truck and got into the driver's side. He looked over at me and pulled out the ring. With the ring in his left hand, he lifted my left hand with his right hand.

He looked me deep in the eyes and whispered, "Stefani, this ring is a promise. A promise to love you and care for you. A promise to wait for you. A promise to marry you when I return from Iraq. Will you wear this ring?" He'd never looked so serious.

"Of course," and he pushed the ring over my knuckle onto my finger. I've never been a ring person or really a promise ring kind of person. When you get a promise from the man you love, you'll wear anything to hold that memory with you indefinitely.

There is nothing quite like being in love. From the beginning, our relationship felt easy. Travis was the first guy with whom I felt I could be completely myself. More than that, the more of me I showed him, the more he adored me. I didn't have to play games or overthink things. I just acted how I wanted to. I was me. Even as I write these words, I smile and beam inside. To love and be loved is truly the greatest gift on this earth.

I wasn't always happy and in love though. I dated a lot of losers before I met my husband. I wish I didn't have to go through so many frogs to meet my prince. I was never one for dating. From a young age, I was looking for "the One." When I was 14 years old, I remember making a list of all the traits and attributes of my "dream man."

Now, I know that God is not some genie to be summoned, and when the Bible says, "ask and you shall receive," it's within a much larger context. Also, His plans come to fruition not for some junior high girl's princess pipedreams, but for the glory of His kingdom. It didn't stop me from meditating on that list a few times a year and constantly wondering when I would get a boyfriend. I assumed that once I had found the One, my life would be set.

"I'll just always be single." I lamented to my mom. It was Christmas 2009. After my first semester of medical school, I was spent.

"Don't say that. Stefani, you're beautiful. You're in medical school. Just be patient. The right guy is waiting for you," my mom encouraged. It never ceased to amaze me that no matter how many times I vented to her, she always listened and tried to cheer me up.

"Yeah, but I've dated a lot of guys, and they all turn out the same," I grumbled. I had become a professional dater, but when nothing lasts beyond the third date, it gets rather lonely. And exhausting.

"Well, it only takes one." She was right.

I met Travis one month later.

I wish I could tell you that this kind of conversation was an exception. Sadly, my family and friends all too often took the brunt of my self-pity over guys. Throughout high school and college, I had wrapped up my sense of worth, beauty, and identity in what guys thought of me. It didn't matter that I was a straight A honors student, an accomplished musician, a gifted athlete, or a spiritual woman. I formed the belief early on that I must have a man to be satisfied.

While Travis can and does make me incredibly happy, he can also make me angry and sad. As with any great romance, the honeymoon phase did end. I love Travis dearly, but when the lose-yourself-in-daydreaming feelings of first love faded, it seemed as though my heart faded as well. I remember the first real fight Travis and I had.

"Stefani, what's wrong?" Valerie placed her hand on my back in the study carrel. She was concerned. She clearly saw my face was red and my eye makeup was smeared from crying. I wasn't fooling anyone.

"Travis and I had a fight," was all I could get out. I continued to cry silently, hoping not to disturb the rest of the medical students studying. It was exam time. After this week, we had three whole weeks off for the holidays. We all needed the break. You could cut the stress in the air with a knife.

"Wh... what happened? Didn't he just get home?" She looked at me confused.

"Yeah." I shrugged. He came home yesterday after four months of deployment. He surprised me at the front door of my apartment. I nearly fell over in disbelief. I'm not an easy one to surprise, but he definitely did it. He took me off guard. After a beautiful day together yesterday and this morning, my nerves got to me. We had our first big fight. For reasons I'll leave unmentioned, Travis had hurt me. I snapped and before I knew it, I kicked him out and retreated to the library to study.

"Well, I'm sure everything will be okay," Valerie comforted. *Shhhhh...* our classmate shushed us from the next study carrel.

"I don't know. I've never been so angry at him before," I whispered. "I mean, I feel so stupid. I thought he was going to propose whenever he came home," I admitted. It was hard pining for someone on deployment when you didn't officially have confirmation that your relationship was forever.

"Well, I know. I know he'll propose," she assured me. I wondered if she knew something I didn't know. Travis knew I didn't want a big, flashy proposal. And even though he never talked to Valerie, she always knew the scoop, even about deployed boyfriends.

"We'll see" I shrugged again and returned to my syllabus. I couldn't concentrate. Tears kept flowing down my face. I felt physically sick to my stomach. Was this it? Was this how he was going to treat me forever? Had he come home to surprise me only to now break up with me?

Half an hour passed when I heard a familiar voice from behind me.

"Hey." Amazing how with one word he could make me weak in the knees.

"Hey." I turned to look up at him behind me. His eyes were red. *Had he been crying too?* He leaned down next to me. He clasped his hands over my hand.

"Stefani, I'm so sorry—" He paused. A tear fell down my cheek. He wiped it away. "I never want to hurt you. I love you. I love you *so* much. Can I please stay with you? I have nowhere else to go." His kind eyes so sincere, so tender.

"Yes." I kissed him softly on the lips. He pulled me up and embraced me.

That weekend, he proposed.

Life, I am certain, is a bunch of messy moments strung together with sweet, loving moments. We dream of the romantic comedy-inspired sweetness, but really, we get mostly mundane with a splash of exhilaration here and there. We're not supposed to be on top of the world all the time, or else being on top of the world wouldn't be special. We also don't need to be on a never-ending rollercoaster.

I was on a rollercoaster before I met my husband. I wish I could take back all the messy tears I cried for stupid boys. I wish I had not placed so much of my emotional stability in the emotional instability of romance. When you place your entire happiness on a man—or any other one person—you will face many letdowns. I wish I hadn't allowed the state of my heart to be defined by a guy. Not only is that an unfair burden to place on a man, but it's also unfair to yourself; to only allow yourself to be you when you're with a man will lead to inevitable heartbreak, whether you are single or not. In the first few years of our relationship, I was still a rollercoaster of emotions. When things were good, I was happy. When things were bad, I was sad. I was short to anger and obsessively worrying. And every emotion in between.

Another thing happens when we invest our sense of self with the men in our lives: we lose ourselves. We naturally are responders and people pleasers, so even the most rebellious of us want to please our husbands. It is normal to intermingle with our husbands, boyfriends, and lovers. Experts call this "fusion," where part of ourselves becomes intertwined with the other. You will lose part of your heart, but you will also gain a part of his heart in the process. You will ebb and flow through each other, but you still retain your core. It's when you forsake your heart without anything in return, or when you give more of yourself than you are prepared to release, that you slowly forget where your relationship ends and you begin.

A Note on Sex

I can't conclude a chapter on relationships without bringing up the elephant in the room: sex. Sex means lots of things to lots of people: fun, recreation, release, and love. While I don't push my beliefs on anyone, I challenge you to look at how sex may be hindering you from bigger issues underneath.

Somehow, our culture has misconstrued the highest expression of love into a casual source of manipulation and coercion.

The amount of jokes that insinuate that women can control men through sex is sad. And while men are visual creatures and sex is generally more vital for men than women, the idea that sex should be used as a form of oppression from any angle is heartbreaking.

Sex has become a Band-Aid for much deeper issues, both personal and societal. Since we can only control ourselves, any change must be within us and in our own sexual relationships. When we cloak our relationship issues with sex and attempt to feed the inner longings of our heart through sex, we miss out on uncovering what sex means to us at all.

It was Valentine's Day, 2014. Our babysitter was spending the night at our house to look after Kate, now almost 10 months old. Travis and I had driven into the city for a romantic night at the Jefferson Hotel. We arrived at our hotel a few hours before our dinner reservations. As we walked in, the warmth comforted me from the stark cold outside. It had been snowing the fluffy, pretty kind of snow that I had become accustomed to in D.C. There was just a trace of snow stuck to the ground, setting a quaint winter backdrop for what felt like our first date.

I glanced up at Travis. He was dressed sharply in his dark gray suit, his purple button-down peeking out of his black leather jacket. He looked down at me. Our eyes met. He gave me butterflies in my stomach, a momentary déja vu from the first time we met. His thumb traced over my knuckles in his hand. He squeezed my hand once, twice, three times, communicating a silent *I love you*. He released my hand to go check in at the front desk. I separated from him, lingering by the artwork on the walls.

The Jefferson is a historic, picturesque, five-star hotel. It is filled with the unique charm of colonial days and the energy of modern times. I couldn't think of a more perfect place to be. Hotels were not foreign to Travis and myself. We spent the first nine months of our marriage geographically separated. Travis was stationed at Fort Hood, Texas while I was finishing medical school in San Antonio. In our honeymoon bliss, we couldn't always wait until the weekend to see each other. Some of my favorite memories were spent driving halfway and meeting in Austin. We would bar hop the famous 6th Street, or we would lounge at a wine bar.

But this hotel was nothing like I'd ever seen. It was breathtaking. Our suite was no exception. There were heated floors in the bathroom, a television screen in the mirror, plush furniture and ambient lighting throughout. If I had a wet dream, it would probably include this suite. I slowly took off my long, cream pea coat. I only wore the coat for extra special occasions, since I was petrified I would spill something on it. I always felt sexy in that coat, like my inner Grace Kelly was shining through. There was so much built up into this night. I felt it. He felt it.

This is supposed to be the part of the book where I share scandalous sexual details about what transpired over the next hour. Out of respect for my reserved hubby and to save scarring my children who may read this book in the future, I'll leave the juicy details to your imagination. I'll just say, sometimes you do get the kind of love that only appears in romance novels. Yet, no matter how intimate the touch, antidepressants can be the ultimate killjoy. If you thought your lack of libido from depression was bad, try the side effects from common antidepressants. You're in for ultimate disappointment in the bedroom.

Needless to say, I did not handle my perceived bodily failure well. After weeks of looking forward to this night out, I was crushed. Moreover, I felt as though I was failing Travis.

"Hey babe, it's okay. We have a lifetime together," he encouraged. If you've ever wrapped your sense of self into the action of sex, you know the feeling of inadequacy that can arise when the action doesn't match the expectations.

Sex can be a beautiful expression of love, a mingling of souls, and a lighthearted release. Nonetheless, even in the most supportive, encouraging partnerships, sex can not only be the result of some underlying problem, but it can also be a source of future self-defeat. It is complicated to remove our personal value and worthiness from the behavior of sexual activity.

Sex and romance can be the trickiest waters to survey. Whether through cultural upbringing or societal influence, we all likely have underlying beliefs about sex and romantic relationships. I address this topic early, because I see women lose themselves in relationships all the time, and the loss of self is subtle. It may take years to realize how much you have changed due to your relationship. Being the you that you want to be in a relationship is a beautiful thing, not to be taken lightly.

I'll leave you with one last thought to ponder. Have you ever thought that the reason you fell in love with your partner had very little to do with him as a person and, instead, how you are around him? Why do we fall in love? Because we love who we are when we are with someone. It is how they make us feel, not necessarily all the details of that person. Our relationships are essentially about our hearts, not the other person.

Find Your HEART

- ♥ **Here and Now.** Replay a recent emotionally charged conversation with your significant other. What thoughts were running through your head?
- ♥ **Embrace Your Emotions.** What emotions or feelings arose in that moment?
- ♥ **Analyze Your Thoughts.** What could your thoughts and feelings be communicating to you about your relationship as a whole?
- ♥ **Reflect On Your Past.** When do you first remember thinking or feeling this way? Do you recall witnessing similar interactions between your own parents?
- ♥ **Take Action.** Share your heart with your husband. Use first person statements, like "I feel" and "I need." State your needs clearly and matter-of-factly.

13
It's Not About the Food

In the construction of this book, this was my last chapter to write. I put off writing it for weeks and took two whole days off before I mustered the courage to write this chapter.

I avoided this chapter like the plague, because of the difficulty in confronting my own pain and weakness in this area, and the weight of feeling the burden of millions of women worldwide. I imagined this book without the inclusion of this chapter. I knew that I would be lying by omission if I published this book without including one of the biggest, if not the biggest, hindrances to women's joy, peace, and sanity. Unfortunately, we have become like goldfish who have forgotten what it means to be wet. We have been swimming in the murkiness of diet culture for so long, probably a lifetime, and we cannot even see the light. My own issues began from a young age.

When I was young, my life revolved around gymnastics. I spent at least four days a week at the gym and begged my parents to take me on the weekends whenever possible. Gymnastics was my ultimate joy, my obsession. For several years, food was never a problem for me. I grew up with food abundance and enjoyed a healthy relationship with food, and my body was never a subject of conversation. Until it was.

I still remember gymnastics coaches commenting on my butt and comparing me to fellow teammates. This is the first of many memories where my body was not only being compared to others but also judged by others. Instead of focusing on the functionality of my body, I grew up with a belief that the aesthetic of my body is what mattered. Maybe had I fallen in love with a less image-centric sport as a child, I could have avoided the plague of body hatred. Yet, seeing as though every single woman I know has been on a diet at one point in time and is currently dissatisfied with their bodies, it was only a matter of time before the crisis with my body began. Unfortunately, other than gymnastics, my other childhood past time was cheerleading, another sport where body aesthetics seem to matter more than anything else.

I remember being called into my music teacher's class after recess. The teacher proceeded to ridicule me for wearing my cheerleading uniform that was "too short" for school policy, and then proceeded to tell me that "shaking my butt" during recess was "unacceptable." For the record, it was school pep rally before a football game. I was doing a cheer with the entire cheerleading squad and was dressed like every other cheerleader. Not to mention, I was the only girl who was called to speak to the music teacher of all people about this harmless act.

Being the impressionable 11-year-old that I was, I did not make the connection that this teacher had obvious issues of her own, and somehow my behavior was bringing to rise her own deep-seeded pain. Instead, I internalized that I was unacceptable. It is one of a few striking moments that I felt my body was being policed by adults around me and that there was something wrong with me.

"I didn't get picked to be flyer," I moaned.

"Why not? You'd be a great flyer! Who did they choose?" my mom accused.

"Lindsay." I was defeated. Absurd as it sounds, being flyer is synonymous with ultimate value in the cheerleading world. For me, it was the goal. I loved gymnastics and acrobatics. The idea of being flyer meant that I could utilize my gymnastics skills outside of the gym. Somehow, I believed in my young 11-year-old brain that I had the power to accomplish this goal, even though it was entirely outside of my control.

"Mom..." I continued.

"Yes?"

"Am I bigger than Lindsay?" I questioned. I was reliving the events of the day, being lined up next to my entire cheerleading squad, one of two girls chosen out of the lineup and compared to my counterpart, as if being the smallest on the team was the ultimate victory, the paramount prize.

"Stefani, you're tiny... it's just..." She paused no doubt searching for the right words to encourage me while also being honest with me. "You're just built different." *Different.* * The one word that no pre-pubescent or adolescent girl wants to be. In an effort to fit in—or rather, make our bodies fit in—we do the only thing that we can think of to fit into the societal standard. We diet.

Dieting

I went on my first diet when I was 13 years old. As young as that sounds, it's actually later than today's average age 11. I was in summer school taking advanced history so that I didn't have to take it during the school year. Like many of my classes at

---

* For the record, the classic beauty icons of history (Audrey Hepburn, Marilyn Monroe, Twiggy, Jennifer Lopez, Kim Kardashian) were characterized as different before they became known as beautiful. Beauty is not only in the eye of the beholder, but also, a sign of cultural and societal standards of a time.

that time, I was the youngest in the class. Not only do I have a summer birthday, but because I was always testing out of classes and trying to get ahead academically, I was often a year younger than my peers. I always felt different. In some regards, I liked it. Being different academically made me feel smart and powerful. Being different physically, though, made me feel unworthy and less valuable.

I judged my internal sense of worth based on whether or not a boy liked me or gave me attention. When I didn't get asked out, I would let it affect my entire psyche. My mind flowed with thoughts, myths, and lies that tied me down. Clearly, this was never about the food or my body. Instead of uncovering the real pain and hurt behind it all, I controlled my food and my body. I went on more diets. I stole diet pills from the store before I was 18 years old. I overdosed on said diet pills in an effort to fix myself "quicker." I watched infomercials for workout equipment and dreamed of the day I would turn 18 and could call the number on the screen and purchase them myself. I assumed that once I had this equipment, I would then finally be able to fix my body.

Then, I went off to college. I felt the pressure of my pre-medicine classes and struggled to fit in. While I had always had friends and family, I now was on my own. Initially, the newness of college brought some relief to my incessant fixation on my body. Quickly, though, the image-centric, female-dominant campus of Baylor University brought me down. Triggered once again by a desire to fit in, my chronic dieting and body hatred peaked into a full-blown eating disorder. Without going into the details of my behaviors (and possibly triggering you reading this), I can attest to wasting days and weeks of my precious college years in perpetual self-destruction. If I wasn't avoiding my friends to engage in destructive behaviors, I was swimming in a swamp of muddled thoughts, obsessions, and irrational beliefs.

Like many, I lived in perpetual pursuit of a future fantasy version of me. The future fantasy version of me who had the perfect body, perfect boyfriend, and perfect grades. *If only I could reach this desired destination*, I thought. I simplified my complex, ever-mounting stress of school into the simple dissatisfaction with my body, and I distilled the solution: do whatever it takes to change my body. I was so steeped in this twisted way of thinking that I never could define the real issue. The real issue is never really about the food. I only wish I had learned that sooner. For nearly ten years, this was my life. I assumed once I could change my body and find a solution that "worked," then everything would unfold. No matter what anyone said—not my parents, not my brothers, not my friends, not even my husband—nothing helped change the ache residing deep inside of me.

Even after getting married, I dreamed of never having girls. I didn't want to deal with the drama of body insecurity and the aesthetic pressures on young girls. I realized I was only avoiding my own internalized pain. The only way I could raise a confident and capable daughter was to regain confidence within myself. Having a daughter is a daily journey through a minefield. Because I know how vulnerable young girls can be and how impressionable I was myself, I am terrified of saying the wrong thing. I either don't compliment her enough and instill lack of confidence in her body, or I compliment her too much and instill pride and self-worth associated *only* with her body. I feel damned if I do, damned if I don't.

Due to a myriad of forces at play, the majority of women are dissatisfied with their bodies. All dieting begins from a dissatisfaction with our bodies. Dieting has become a core hobby, and the desire to change our bodies has become an obsession. We have become disillusioned to think that we have it within our control to alter our bodies, and that we can predict how we will feel when we do alter our bodies. Furthermore, we believe that we must be striving for ideal bodies in the first place. We have drunk the Kool-Aid that is the diet industry, which feeds us flawed arguments: (1) weight loss is necessary for health, (2) we are only worthy when we are at our "ideal weight," and (3) we must do whatever it takes to pursue this ideal, fantasy version of ourselves.

While I could go on about the harms of dieting and explain how dieting is quite possibly the most destructive thing you could ever do to yourself physically and emotionally, I will save it for a future book. I will challenge you to look beyond food and your body. None of your dieting and fitness obsessions are about the food. Think of what is beneath the dieting. For myself and many others, control over our food is synonymous with the desire to control our lives. Since dieting is more culturally accepted than drugs, alcohol, or other addictions, it has become a core coping skill for millions of women nationwide (and could even be your only coping skill).

Like other coping skills, it's a temporary fix, a fleeting behavior to redirect your mind from distress or to avoid intense emotional pain. I'm not suggesting that eating in and of itself is an avoidance technique, though it can be. I'm stating that dieting and the obsessive thinking about your body, weight, and food is more than likely a signal to a deeper issue, the smoke signal for the forest fire. As I've already said, and I'll say it again, *it's not about the food*. If you can gently begin to question what drives these behaviors, you can connect with the root cause of your dieting or your incessant desire to change your body.

Plastic Surgery

If dieting is alluring, plastic surgery is intoxicating. The promise of the ideal body, no matter your flaws, is seductive. But we know that plastic surgery doesn't really change anything, which is likely why the majority of women who have one procedure will go on to have more procedures, constantly chasing the illusory change that will never come.

After having a daughter, I struggled to accept my postpartum body. For the record, research shows that postpartum depression and body dissatisfaction are highly intertwined. If having a baby alone wasn't enough of a trigger for disordered thoughts around food and my body, the postpartum depression definitely was.

I had an inkling that this was not about food or my body, but I continued to avoid the deeper issue behind my fixation on my body. I had tried countless diets and various workout programs. Nothing really "worked," as in, nothing caused lasting, permanent change in my body, and certainly nothing caused permanent change in my mind. On some level, I knew I needed a solution, a *permanent* solution. So I sought out plastic surgery.

"Hello, this is Dr. D's plastic surgery center, how may I help you?" The receptionist picked up the phone.

"Yeah… um… I'm interested in plastic surgery?" It was more of a question than a statement. I was already regretting this phone call.

"Well, what kind of procedure are you interested in?" She sounded so chipper yet calming. No wonder this surgeon had all the best reviews. His office staff was already comforting, and I'd only been on the phone for five seconds.

"Um, I'm not sure, I just had a baby and—"

"Oooh!!!" she interrupted, "You'll definitely want to hear about our Mommy Makeover package."

"Okay?" I already knew this was a bad idea.

"So, our Mommy Makeover includes breast augmentation, which may or may not include a breast lift and tummy tuck with liposuction," she said proudly.

"Okay." Clearly my brain had stopped working. I was having an out of body experience. This is not me. I remember having fully-heated arguments over the futility of plastic surgery in my Bioethics class in college. Now, here I was, on the phone requesting a plastic surgery consult. *Who was I?*

"I've had the procedure myself. The breast augmentation, lift, and tummy tuck, that is. And I must say, it is incredible! Dr. D is the best…" she continued. *She must have experience furthering conversation with doubtful women on the line*, I thought. She went on to explain the nuts and bolts of the procedure itself, pain management, what to expect with regard to healing, recovery, and returning to daily routines.

"And what if I want to have more children?" I just had Kate. I knew I wanted more children. Why I was considering plastic surgery after the birth of only one baby is beyond me, though it shows how pervasive the body-hate messaging is, especially with new mothers. If I couldn't get my ideal body through diet and exercise (like I'd already tried), then I would need to permanently change my body to achieve the look that I wanted.

"Well, ma'am, while we are in the business of making money, we really do view this as an investment," she asserted. *The business of making money*, I thought. *Off of women's insecurities*, I added. *An investment?*

"What do you mean an investment?" I already knew that procedures don't last forever. Breast augmentations require ongoing maintenance. Fat reallocation is a fairly common "complication" of liposuction. Removing fat in one location doesn't mean that fat will not return in the same location or different location.

"This is an investment in your future. And as an investment, it requires care and maintenance over the years. We recommend MRIs every 10 years with silicone breast implants. And many women continue to require liposuction indefinitely." *Require? Is she saying that women just continue to gain weight even after liposuction?*

"Okay, well, let me think it over." I had already thought it over.

"All right, well, our holiday spots fill up quickly, so if you want to get on the wait list, let us know as soon as possible." I didn't. "Thank you." And I hung up.

There is nothing inherently wrong with plastic surgery. I have many friends who are plastic surgeons, and I know friends who have had plastic surgery. I'm not even opposed to plastic surgery for myself one day. The problem, like many details of life, is in the mindset behind the plastic surgery. If you are like many, you consider plastic surgery as the Holy Grail to the perfect body. With that perfect body, you can then have amazing sex, a fulfilling home life, well-behaved children, your dream home, and an ideal life. But it's not about your body.

What if I told you that none of that would change just because your body changes? Sure, you may get a few more looks from men, and you may even be treated better at work. For a time. After a while, things will return just as they were, and you are left once again with what is. If this whole time you have withered your mental energy in pursuit of some ideal, fantasy version of you, it will be a painful rude awakening when you realize that you are still you. Ordinary. Normal. Real.

It took me a very long time to be okay with my "ordinary" body. After almost two decades of body hatred, I have finally reached a place of respect—and daresay, love—for my body. I no longer diet. I do not follow a meal plan. I do not buy into "guidelines" or food rules. I don't weigh myself. I don't count macros. I believe God divinely created my body to know when, what, and how much to eat to nourish my body so that I can continue living on this earth.

I also know that, at the end of the day, any external benchmark will never satisfy an internal need. For anyone interested in truly making permanent change with food and their bodies, I recommend starting with *Intuitive Eating* by Evelyn Tribole and Elise Resch, *Health at Every Size* by Linda Bacon, and *Body Kindness* by Rebecca Scritchfield. These books, along with professional therapy and a big dose of self-compassion, transformed my mindset. Truly, food is just food. My body is just the agent to help me live God's purpose for my life. I no longer obsess about calories, macros, or my scale.

Hear me out. I know how radical I may sound right now. I know it is also somewhat annoying to hear from someone who "has it all together" around food and her body. I encourage you. This took me more than a decade to learn. A decade! Not days, weeks, or months. Years. Now I act with kindness and love for my body. Out of respect for His Creation, I will never go back to my body-loathing, food-obsessed, workout-possessed days. *Ever.* I share this, because I want you to know that there is a light, and that light is not at the end of the diet tunnel. It's when you get out of the tunnel altogether.

Find Your *HEART*

- ❤ **Here and Now.** What thoughts arise when you think about food and your body?
- ❤ **Embrace Your Emotions.** How do you feel about your body? (For the record, fat is not a feeling. When you say to yourself, "I feel fat," what physical sensation are you trying to describe? Get specific.)
- ❤ **Analyze Your Thoughts.** What could your thoughts and feelings about your body be communicating to you about your life as a whole?
- ❤ **Reflect On Your Past.** When do you first remember feeling this way?
- ❤ **Take Action.** Do one small thing to care for your personal needs right now.

For more help with food and body image issues, check out my free training at www.notaboutthefood.com.

14
Look Beyond Your Material Goods

I don't know how my parents did it. Two middle class working people gave my brothers and me everything they had to give: private music lessons, lavish birthday parties, elaborate family vacations, stylish clothes, dance classes, gymnastics, golf memberships, elite summer camps, private college education, and more. They never had a lot to spare. We never received financial support from extended family or friends. My parents demonstrated the epitome of grace.

My childhood was similar to many, with two working parents who generally lived paycheck to paycheck and gave most of their earnings to their children. My family also had the added burden of a small business. My dad owned a restaurant from the time I was 10 years old, and I started working there from the beginning. When I was too young to hostess or wait tables, I would clean restrooms or help my dad file paperwork. Restaurant business may not have been my favorite job, but I did enjoy making my own money. I was able to pay for clothes, gas, gifts, and entertainment with friends when I was in high school without having to ask my parents. I paid my own sorority dues and some living expenses when I was in college.

While making money built confidence and self-sufficiency within me, I also saw the dark side of money, witnessing several heated arguments between my parents. As the only daughter—and very likely the most expensive child—I was often the root of the financial stress. Unknowingly, I internalized several limiting beliefs regarding money.

First, money is bad. When money is associated with hard work or fighting, it's a concrete thought that money is bad. Furthermore, I am bad for having or wanting money. We are all fed the same line: money is the root of all evil. We rarely challenge this thinking. Yet, particularly in evangelical circles, we wrongly associate all money with evil. As such, we unconsciously hinder any wealth that may come our way. In an effort to uphold our morality, we stunt our financial growth before it even begins. Worse, we squander away any financial blessings that may come our way. Money is neither evil or sinful. We can argue about the intentions behind money, but money itself just is. It is neither positive nor negative. It is neutral. To remove the high charge of emotions associated with money is freeing.

Next, money leads to conflict. Practically the only thing I ever saw my parents fight about was money. Because of this, I easily associated having money with leading to conflict. I'm not alone in this. The number one cause of marital conflict, and therefore divorce, is finances. Additionally, financial stressors remain an extremely common cause of suicide and mental health decline. It's understandable when we realize that the majority of us, men or women, wrap up our self-worth in our monetary wealth.

Lastly, I am not worth it. This is not specific to money per say but general to life. This belief took me a long time to uncover, but I quickly observed that I am not alone in this limitation. Several patients, friends, and acquaintances that I have encountered also feel on some fundamental level that they are not worth it. Not worth spending money on. Not worth elaborate gifts being given to them. Not worth chivalry by a man. Not worth success. Not worth love. Not worth abundant satisfaction in life.

"I can't do it anymore," Laura declared as she plopped down on the couch in my office.

"Can't do what?" Perplexed, I turned from my desk to face her. She was five minutes early for her appointment. The administrative staff must have let her walk back to my office because she seemed irritated.

"This! Us. You and me. Therapy. I can't do it anymore." She crossed her arms and looked down at the ground.

"Okayyy," I was lost. Laura was one of my most stable patients. She was always on time, paid in advance, and had told me on multiple occasions how beneficial therapy was for her.

"I just can't," she repeated. She uncrossed her arms and began fiddling with her fingers and then intertwined them in her lap.

"Well, I will respect whatever you decide. Since you are here already and you've paid for this session, why don't we first discuss what is on your mind today?"

"John and I had a fight again today." Her voice had calmed down now.

"Oh yeah?" I wasn't entirely shocked. She and John were always fighting. John traveled a lot for his job as a consultant. She recently had a miscarriage and felt alone. They did not communicate their needs well with each other.

"Yeah… I know you're probably getting sick of hearing about our fights. I should just bring him in here and maybe he could tell you all about it."

"What would John be able to say that you couldn't tell me yourself?"

"Well, he's pissed about the lease."

"What about the lease?"

"I've never put John's name on the lease."

"Oh." I was taken aback. They had lived together three years. I assumed that they shared a lease agreement.

"Yeah… I don't know. After my ex, I—" she stopped herself. She had been in an eight-year relationship prior to her current relationship. Her ex-fiancé had cheated on her multiple times. She still hadn't fully processed the pain. "I never want to give a guy that power over me again, I guess," she admitted.

"Sounds like it," I confirmed.

"It never really comes up either. We each pay our share of the bills," she explained.

"But…?" I sensed she wasn't telling me something.

"But he hasn't paid the last three months of his portion of the rent. I got a notice today of being past due. They'll issue an eviction notice if we don't pay them by the end of this week." She let out a sigh. She took a few deep breaths and made eye contact with me. Tears began to well in her eyes.

"I see the burden you feel in your eyes," I reflected. And I could. The burden of her financial distress was weighing down my entire office. "What holds you back from asking John for his share of the rent?"

"I just feel bad," she stated. If I had a nickel for every time some woman said "I feel bad," I'd be a wealthy woman.

"Do you feel bad because he hasn't paid rent? Or do you feel bad about possibly hurting his feelings by asking him to pay rent?"

"Both, I guess."

"Which one?"

Laura was silent for a while. Silent tears were now flowing down her cheeks. "I just feel like he doesn't love me, and him not paying his rent just cements the fact that he doesn't care," she concluded. *She had equated money with love.*

After a few more minutes of discussing her relationship troubles, I could feel her anxiety rising once again.

"What's on your mind?" I reframed.

"I just feel I'm spending too much money on therapy. That's all." *Or she felt like she was spending too much money on herself.*

"What makes you feel that way?"

"I don't know. It's really just a lot of money."

I cannot deny that therapy is expensive. But I knew that it was never about the money to begin with. "I understand it is an investment to afford therapy with me. Do you feel like you are not worth that investment?" I confronted her with the deeper issue.

"What do you mean?" she questioned.

"Do you feel like you are worth the investment?" I probed.

"Maybe not," she admitted sheepishly.

"Let's explore that," I suggested.

Laura was able to open up that she had equated money with love. While growing up, both her parents worked and she was an only child. She received a lot of presents and money from her parents but not the love and affection she desired. Her romantic relationships were similar. Ironically, though she equated money with love, she also held the limiting belief that she was not worthy of love, so thereby, she was not worthy of money.

I have treated billionaires and homeless people and everyone in between. I have family and friends from just about every walk of life as well. One thing remains clear: how we feel about money has very little to do with how much or how little we have. It's our mindset behind the money itself that creates a feeling of satisfaction. Rich people can have a scarcity mindset, and poor people can have an abundance mindset. Wealthy people can be just as miserable over money as homeless people. Those who have very little can be some of the most content people I know, while those who have plenty can also have a tremendous guilt mindset.

How you view money also predicts what you will do with money. For instance, if you believe that you will never have enough, then you will likely live in debt, invest poorly, and spend frugally. In essence, you will prove yourself correct: you never do have enough. On the contrary, if you believe that you have abundantly more than you need (which the overwhelming majority of us do), you will live comfortably, invest adequately, and not be afraid of generous giving.

While I have never reached billionaire status, I have been abundantly blessed financially. When I first started making a real doctor's salary, you know what happened? Nothing. Absolutely nothing changed. I still wore the same clothes, paid the same bills, and purchased the same food brands. The fact that I'm still paying more than my mortgage in student loans each month may have something to do with it. I'll also say that money does not change us. The fantasy selves we imagine will arise when we make a lot of money do not exist.

We envision that money will bring us a new life with new hobbies, interests, and passions. Like a new body, more money has been attached to all kinds of emotions: happiness, fulfillment, joy, love, and peace. Yet, without changing the underlying beliefs about money, nothing will actually change.

Our beliefs about money do not change overnight. Our beliefs will stay with us whether we have a lot or a little. As I reflect on my many different financial states of my life, my feelings around money have not changed much in my life. I'm grateful for amazingly generous parents who showed an example of grace. Still, I co-opted a scarcity mindset. Marketing experts and business ploys will feed on scarcity. To combat scarcity requires daily practice in gratefulness and abundance. Once again, we must give up the futuristic fantasy. Focus on what is, instead of what is not.

Look Past the Things

"Are you okay, ma'am?" the tow truck driver called out. I shrugged. "I think you might be bleeding." I touched my nose. *He was right. I did have a nosebleed. Why was my nose bleeding?*

"Uh, yeah, I think… I'm good." I puttered over my words. I looked over at Kate safely nestled in her car seat, not even a cry. She was still, silent, smiling up at me.

"How is she doing? You need me to call an ambulance? I mean, I want to make sure y'all are all right. That was quite a contact." He was referring to my PT cruiser crashing into the off-ramp rail when we tried to make an exit too quickly.

"How fast were you going, sir?" I heard the officer ask Travis from a distance.

"I'm not sure, I know the brakes aren't that good. We've been needing to get them fixed." Travis answered. *Nice call, Travis. You didn't mention the fact that your wife was nagging you with directions for the past 10 minutes and screamed for you to take the exit.*

I heard the officer walk around inspecting the scene. "I see the tire marks. Your breaks were working pretty well, so it seems." Well, the breaks had been an issue for a while but they usually acted up only in the rain.

"Yeah…" Travis mumbled. He couldn't reply. The officer was right. He had been speeding and took a risky turn. *No thanks to my cajoling, mind you.*

"You sure you're okay, ma'am?" The tow truck driver urged. "I can easily call the ambulance. It's really no big—"

"No…" I cut him off. "We're fine," I said firmly. "But thank you." He was very kind after all. But I knew what an ambulance meant. It meant an emergency room visit that would take the rest of the day and well into the night for them to check me and Kate out. And we didn't have any visible injuries. I had been in the backseat. The airbag hadn't even activated. The nosebleed was likely just a stress response or reaction to the dry winter. I was fine. Kate was safe. Travis wasn't injured either.

Travis made his way back to the car. "You guys okay?"

I nodded. Inside, I'm thinking, *Well, no, I'm not okay. You totaled my car because of my nagging. And now, I have no clue how I'll make my shifts in the ER the rest of the month. Better yet, I don't know how we will afford another car right now.*

"Well, I guess that answers that," Travis joked. He was referring to whether or not we needed a new car and when we would be able to buy a new car.

"Yep, guess so," I replied.

I had driven the PT Cruiser for the past 10 years. I'm not a big car person, so I didn't have some love affair with it. In fact, I'd been wanting a new car for a long time. Between childcare and student loans, my residency salary couldn't stretch to afford a car payment. Ironically, we were on our way to look at used cars so that we could budget expenses for the next few months to afford a new one. After totaling my car though, I had no choice; I needed a new car now.

Over the next few days, we shopped around and settled on a certified pre-owned 2013 gray Mazda CX-5, the car I drive currently. I love so many things about this car: Bluetooth, sunroof, heated leather seats. I've become so accustomed to the comforts of my car, I cannot believe I was able to drive my PT cruiser for as long as I did. Although it's not a Lexus, BMW, or other high-end vehicle, I freaking love my car.

When I first started driving it, I would take extra special care. I wouldn't eat in my car, I'd protect the seats when our dog Trooper rode in the car with us, and I would vacuum weekly, with regular deluxe car washes. I loved seeing the pristine condition of my car. Commuting in Washington, DC traffic, I spent a lot of time in it.

A funny thing happened though. The longer I owned my car, the easier it was to forget about it. I stopped vacuuming regularly and didn't wash it routinely. I ate in it, Kate spilled in it, and Trooper shed in it. And I stopped taking care of it. That's the thing with things. After a momentary high, we quickly lose interest. We become conditioned to it being in our lives. We no longer take extra special care.

About a year later, my iPhone 4 began acting up. People on the other line couldn't hear me. I couldn't hear them. It was incredibly frustrating. I took it to the Apple store. They said it was the internal microphone, which would cost more than the phone was worth itself. I totaled my iPhone.

Now, I remember when I first got my iPhone 4. Heck, I remember when I first got a cell phone! With an iPhone, I was ahead of the curve of most of my friends who were still using BlackBerries or flip phones. I purchased the iPhone with my own money from bartending at my dad's restaurant, and I could not have been more proud of myself.

When I totaled my phone, all I could think of was getting a new phone. I didn't care about the memories of when I first purchased my iPhone. I didn't have heartache over the particular thing. I had heartache over the lack of functionality that the thing provided me. As swiftly as I broke my phone, I picked out a new phone and carried on.

For most of us, things are just that: things. They serve a limited purpose for a limited time. My car serves a means of transportation. My iPhone serves as a means of communication. For some though, things can truly hinder our spirit and prevent us from delving to the depths of our pain or our hurt.

A patient of mine, Rachel, was a pathological, clinical hoarder. She had been evicted from two previous residences and had been court-ordered to therapy to deal with her hoarding behaviors.

"I got rid of one box this week," Rachel beamed.

"That's great!!!" I get pretty excited for my patients. Most therapists feel it's breaking form to show emotion, but I think most people don't have others in their lives who get excited *enough*. So, I get excited.

"Yeah, I'm trying to get my son's help to come get it." Rachel often cited her son as a prime instigator for her need to get rid of things. He had been the one to help her move and put her belongings into four large storage units.

"It's still in your house?" I calmly probed.

"Well, yeah…" she trailed. "But it's all sealed up in a box. I haven't opened it or anything. It's by the front door." Rachel also had agoraphobia, so I knew she didn't leave the house often.

I waited. Sometimes, the right thing to say is nothing at all.

"It had my mom's dishes in there," Rachel admitted. "I put her beautiful china bowls in there. She has others, but this was one set, so I thought I could get rid of them."

Most of Rachel's things were actually her mother's things. She and her mother had a strained relationship, to put it nicely. Rachel was the oldest of five children and bore the brunt of severe physical and emotional abuse from her single mother for most of her childhood. She was the peacemaker of her siblings and handled the majority of drama in the family. She had begun collecting things decades ago. When her mother passed away five years earlier, her hoarding hit an all-time level of destruction. Fire department chiefs and cops had been involved, because her apartments had become "unlivable." This happened not once but twice in the past five years. No matter how many times she started over in a new location, with her things locked up tightly in storage units, she would eventually collect more. By the time she was evicted, she had hoarded even more things.

"And?" I nudged.

"I think I haven't forgiven my mother," she declared. "How could I?" she continued. "She bruised and beat me. She shamed me in front of my family. She was never encouraging. She called me stupid and dumb and ugly. I feel like she destroyed me." I could feel her hurt resonating from her words. She is not alone in her suffering. Despite the countless heartbreaking childhood stories I have heard, I still grieve inside each and every time I hear them.

"But she was your mother," I stated.

"Yes, she was," she agreed.

"How does it feel holding onto her things?" I inquired. I already knew the answer.

"Horrible." She let out an anxious laugh. One thing you learn in therapy: when someone laughs when talking about an otherwise serious manner, you've definitely hit on something.

"Then what are you gaining from holding onto her things?" I knew her things were protecting her in some way. I wanted Rachel to uncover that for herself.

"I'm not sure," she answered honestly.

Depending on the severity or chronicity of hoarding behavior, it can be especially challenging to dig to the heart of the issues at play. An onlooker may easily see *Oh, obviously, she has issues with her mother.* As with most psychodynamic interpretations, it is a fluid hypothesis and an ever-expanding formulation. Unfortunately, Rachel terminated therapy with me a few weeks later. We were never able to finish the work we started.

That's the other thing with things: to minimize your stuff is only the first step. The real work begins once the stuff is stripped away, and we are left with the raw feelings underneath. Handling these much deeper issues is messy. Until you pick up the mess, no amount of simple living will ever solve your problems.

Most of us never reach hoarder level, and most of us also do not have the same level of traumatic pasts. Hoarding occurs when individuals displace the same level of emotion reserved for human relationships onto things. Therefore, getting rid of things is akin to the same hurt of a painful breakup with a lover or the loss of a friend. It's not something easily fixed. Digging to the heart of the matter is the only means of real change, though.

While I don't connect with electronics and cars, I'm not immune to emotional attachment to things. I have struggled with getting rid of clothes, shoes, baby toys, and kitchenware. I still hold on to framed pictures and household décor, even though they collect dust in my closet. And my husband and I both felt sadness when we sold our beautiful mahogany bar. We struggle with releasing things that we have emotional attachments to. Hoarder or not, we all attach emotions to things at some point in our lives.

Clothes that don't fit remind us of a "better body." Baby toys are a sign of growing children. Nice dishes bring us back to hosting parties and entertaining friends. Framed pictures hold our memories. Household décor keep our personalities. And a beautiful bar was a relic of a simpler time, when we were young and in lusty love, unbridled with children and heavy responsibilities of life. While holding onto the things of our past, we miss out on the beauty of what is.

Before our last PCS (permanent change of station, i.e. military move), I caught the minimalism bug. I had already read *The One Thing* and *Essentialism*, and unknowingly had practiced simple living for a couple years, more out of utility than choice. I was now listening to the Minimalists' podcast and reading the blog posts. What began as a standard "PCS purge" became a radical reevaluation of our needs.

We first concluded that we wanted to downsize. For financial reasons and otherwise, we would be downsizing from a 2,500 square-foot townhouse outside Washington, D.C. to a 1,300 square-foot apartment outside Norfolk, VA. We sold our pool table, bar, and leather sofas. We donated clothes, dishes, books, and household items. We got rid of a ton of stuff, literally.

While I sometimes miss the spacious living area and floor-to-ceiling bay windows of our townhouse, I would not trade the simplicity and peace of my life currently for the world. While I still dream of my Texas ranch house one day, I have found peace and contentment with less. Minimalism may not be the silver bullet, but with less things distracting you, the truth is more easily seen. And I realize that things, like everything else, can be the ties that bind our hearts.

Find Your HEART

- **Here and Now.** What thoughts arise when you think about money or material goods?
- **Embrace Your Emotions.** How do you feel about your current financial situation or about the things you have in your possession?
- **Analyze Your Thoughts.** What could your thoughts and feelings about your material goods be communicating to you about your life as a whole?
- **Reflect On Your Past.** When do you first remember thinking or feeling this way?
- **Take Action.** Get rid of one large black trash bag full of material items. Investigate your thoughts and emotions that arise.

15
Doing More, Feeling Less

I used to love to-do lists. I loved planning out my list. I loved dreaming of accomplishing all of my daily to-dos. And I loved the rush that came from crossing something off of my list. I used to add to my list tasks that were already completed, just so I could have the satisfaction of crossing it off my list. I would buy elaborate planners and methodically choose the best electronic applications for recording my mini-achievements.

Think of how little is actually important in your day. Review all of your tasks that "must be done." I used to wear busyness as a badge of honor. It doesn't end with us. These days, we mothers put our children in tons of activities. Where is it getting us? We run on the hamster wheel of life and think that it will bring us to some utopian end where all of our problems are solved, our wounds are healed. Doing more will never amount to feeling better. Never. *Ever.* Read that again and let it sink in.

Adding more to our to-do lists and bringing on more unnecessary errands does not solve any underlying pain or heartache. It is yet another distraction for us. We cover our hearts with more to-dos, because we are afraid of what it is to be.

"I just want to know how to get it all done," Leigh said. Leigh was a former interior designer, turned stay-at-home mom after the birth of her two children.

"What do you mean?" Of course I knew what she meant, but sometimes, it serves patients well for them to hear their thoughts come out of their own mouths rather than mine.

"I don't even know." She held up her hands and chuckled lightly.

"What makes you feel as though you are not getting it all done?" I suggested.

"Haha, because I'm not," she laughed. Her laughter was a sign of some anxiety. I knew this was a good direction.

"Hmm, so what is it that you feel you must get done?" I tried a different approach.

"I don't know… dishes, laundry, cooking. Just stuff, I guess. I don't know, it's just all the motherhood stuff. I'm just not cut out for it," she lamented. It kills me every time women define motherhood with the stuff. I could write an entire book on just that, but I will save my soapbox for another day. For now, I'll only say, motherhood is not about dishes, laundry, grocery shopping, and cooking.

"How do you feel when you can actually get it all done?"

"Well, I don't know…" she started. In case you're wondering, "I don't know" is a fairly common reply I get to my questioning. Truth moment: you do know. You just usually have either conflicting emotions or judgment behind your decision. "I don't know" becomes the catch-all, politically correct response.

"I guess…" she started again. "It's just…" she paused. "I like feeling accomplished."

"And doing more makes you feel accomplished?"

"Yes."

164

"And what would you feel if you didn't complete all of your tasks?"

"Ha... I guess like I do now?" she said more like a question than an answer. Patients are always looking to me to validate what they're saying. There are no right or wrong answers in therapy.

"Which is..." I probed.

"Which is not great. I feel out of control." *Ah the infamous control*, I thought. It's always about control.

"When did you last feel in control?"

"I'm not sure..." she lingered. "I guess when I was working."

Uh huh, I nodded.

"Yeah, I'm not sure if I've ever shared with you before, but I actually really liked work. I liked the projects I worked on and knowing I could get tasks done."

"And the affirmation that came with it?" I presumed.

"Well, yeah, actually, it's nice to be appreciated for the work you've done," she admitted. She seemed a little distraught.

Leigh was an interior designer and a highly sought after one at that. She was used to bringing order, balance, and beauty to physical spaces. She was able to use her creative side as well as her linear thinking to achieve true art in her clients' homes. Usually, her projects ended with not only financial compensation but also the joy of seeing delight and satisfaction on her customers' faces. She gave up her career to stay home with her children three years ago. We had spoken only briefly about her distant career, but I sensed that she missed something about it.

"And you don't feel appreciated as a mother?" I asked.

"Well... no." She laughed as she said it. "Not really, I guess. I don't really expect to either, it's just—"

"It's just hard." I completed her sentence. As a mother, I fully get it. It's probably one of the reasons that I like being a working mother, because I do get some positive feedback in my career, whereas motherhood is purely sacrificial, especially when your kids are very young.

"Yeah…" Leigh began tearing up. Anytime tears are shed or emotions are triggered, I know I've hit a sore spot. Leigh had been treating motherhood like her job. When projects weren't given to her by a boss, she assumed the chores herself. She had been filling her to-do list to be busy. She used busyness to avoid the heart of the issue: mourning the loss of her career.

"I see we've hit a pain point," I bring to her attention.

"Yeah, I'm sorry." I really wish women would stop apologizing for showing emotions. It's a bad habit, ladies. Stop it. "I think I really miss my job," she admitted.

"How could you incorporate your job into your life again?" I pondered. What women don't realize is that even when you decide to stay at home full-time with your children, you can still incorporate the parts of your job that you love into your home.

"Well, we just bought a vacation home. I'm looking forward to fixing that up. And I'm planning to take on a few clients this fall, so that gets me excited!" Her face said it all. The tears had dried up. She looked the most excited I had ever seen her.

"That sounds fabulous. I'm really happy for you." I beamed, hoping she could feel her own positive energy reflecting back.

Leigh's story is a great example. The heart of the matter is never really the thing that's right in front of you. She had been stressing over the tasks and details of her home, when in actuality she was yearning to use her creative talents in her job again, and facing the many complicated emotions that came with that.

We can also commonly use tasks and busyness to avoid the pain and discomfort of deeper issues. We live in an Instant Gratification World, and yet nothing good in life comes overnight. Nothing. In my pre-med years, my classmates and I almost had T-shirts branded with the words "Delayed Gratification." This was a motto—credo, if you will—that helped us get through the hard times. We believed in a light at the end of the tunnel. What I now see is that it's not just medical training that is Delayed Gratification. Almost anything great in life comes with a Delayed Gratification tag. Motherhood, marathon training, fitness and health, startup businesses, and marriage are all a testament to Delayed Gratification.

For most of us, accepting Delayed Gratification is a challenge. We use task lists and milestone markers as a way to keep us busy. Really, what we're doing is avoiding the pain of waiting, the discomfort of boredom. If you ask any person who suffers from addiction or disordered eating, they will tell you that boredom is the most common trigger. Sadly, we are conditioned from a young age to be busy. When I was a young girl myself, I was constantly busy. I never had a free moment. If I wasn't in school, I was in sports practices or music lessons. On the weekends, if I wasn't at gymnastics competitions or golf tournaments, I was in debate tournaments or music recitals. And if I ever sneaked a free weekend in, I would be working at my dad's restaurant.

I prided myself on busyness. I was a master at productivity. The gurus of today pale in comparison to my level of productivity. Still to this day, I am frequently asked how I "do it all." Efficiency is my middle name. But efficiency doesn't give you warm hugs at night. Productivity doesn't take away the pain of losing a loved one. And time management doesn't hold our hand when we cry.

Because challenging our thoughts and feelings is unpleasant, we focus our energy on more busyness. We associate busyness with productivity, productivity with achievement, achievement with acceptance, and acceptance with love. We no longer feel comfortable just being. Just being equates to laziness. Instead, what if we reframed boredom with patience? And patience is what is necessary with Delayed Gratification.

Patience does not come naturally to me. Although I am a doctor who was in school and training for literally 25 years of my life, I am not a patient person. I don't like to wait. When I want something, I want it now. Resisting this impulsive inclination has taken years of mindfulness. I have come to welcome boredom, not as a nuisance, but as a teacher. I now view patience as the bravest act in the world.

When we ask Kate what patience means, she says "to wait for the right time." Waiting for the right time is hard. Being able to wait patiently without filling our plates with tasks and busyness is even more challenging. Being is hard—being present, being in pain—but being is our only escape from the tumultuous burdens that we are placing on ourselves every day. Being is our ticket out of this busyness hell we have created for ourselves, the hell that holds us back from our heart.

On Accomplishments

"Today's the day, right?" my mom asked.

"Well, officially not until tomorrow," I corrected. Tomorrow was Early Match Day for medical schools. For early interviewers, you would hear if you got accepted or not. Whether you matched or not would be posted to the website.

"Why don't we just check? I bet you they tell you today before the weekend," my mom probed. I admit, it was bizarre that Match Day was on a Saturday. I mean, obviously, medical school admissions departments did not work on the weekends. Likely, the lists had already been sent to the administration.

"Okay…" I lingered. A part of me was nervous checking my email in front of my mother. What if I didn't get accepted? After being wait-listed last year and rejected at the last minute, I'd spent a long time waiting. Waiting seemed to be easier to handle than the pain of rejection. Maybe waiting one more day wasn't so bad.

"Just do it," my mom stated, as she sat down next to me in my dad's home office.

I can still feel the nerves in my fingers and the butterflies in my stomach as I share this story with you. It was one of the most anxious moments of my life, with so many conflicting emotions at play. I had spent my entire life wanting to be a doctor. With the exception of my brief fascination with Broadway in high school, I had always known I wanted to be a doctor.

I scrolled to the browser, navigated to my email account, and typed in my username and password. There it was, clear as day in front of me: one unread email from University of Texas Health Sciences Center at San Antonio Admissions Committee.

"I GOT IN!!!" Tears immediately spilled from my eyes.

My mom wailed in excitement. She embraced me. We both jumped for joy. Literally. My dad came rushing back to join us. He heard us screaming.

"She got into UT San Antonio!" my mom exclaimed. It was my first choice. I loved everything about the medical school. I knew it was exactly where I wanted to study medicine. And I got in. I got accepted to medical school. I was going to be a doctor.

My dad started crying. He hugged me. "I'm so proud of you, Snookems." He kissed me on the forehead. We hugged some more. This was the symbol of a lifetime of discipline for me and a lifetime of sacrifice for them.

We celebrated that night as a family. I was flooded with congratulations from family, friends, and acquaintances alike. I was walking on cloud nine. My dad later remarked, "You know, it's pretty special. Not many people can turn a dream into reality. But you did. You did it!" I was grateful beyond measure.

After getting rejected from medical school the previous year, I had been in a funk. I didn't know who I was. I had linked my sense of worth to my achievements, and because I failed, I believed myself to be a failure. I prayed for clarity, that if God wanted me to be a doctor that He would grant me acceptance to medical school. When I was accepted, I felt fierce clarity for the first time in years. I knew this was God's path for my life.

Eight months later, I would stand proudly and receive my white coat at the inaugural White Coat Ceremony, welcoming all incoming medical students. Only in medical training do we honor students before they even begin their training. I'm thankful that we do though. The road to becoming a doctor is a long and arduous path, fraught with valleys, cliffs, and rocks hindering your pass. Being able to celebrate milestones along the way makes the road seem less daunting and offers the brief glimmer of hope that you need to make it through the next stage of training.

Sadly, most achievements in life never obtain the kind of pomp and circumstance granted to soon-to-be-doctors. The path of life is no less challenging than the academic path of becoming a doctor. Yet, we don't throw parties for keeping up your house or paying your bills on time. When strapped by demands of life, these can be insurmountable feats in and of themselves.

We shouldn't have to wait to graduate, get married, have a baby, or start a new job to take joy in our accomplishment, that is, unless the accomplishment is not something that we truly wanted in the first place. If we are accomplishing goals for the sake of accomplishing goals, we will never be fulfilled. If we are reaching for achievements that someone else made for us, we will never connect with who we are and what we want.

I wish I could say that I learned to celebrate more and to savor the small stuff, but I continued to struggle. From the moment I started medical school, I began working on a side hustle. Whether avoiding the challenges of medical school or being unfulfilled in some way, shape, or form, I kept searching for something more outside of myself. I started a blog in medical school when social media marketing was only in its infancy, but never kept it up consistently. More importantly, I was censoring myself, constantly thinking and rethinking everything I put out into the world. Clearly that was never going to be sustainable if fear was hindering my ability to connect. Lesson learned.

Then, after starting residency, I bought into the passive income idea. I knew I "had to have" multiple streams of income.

170

I assumed that if I could only create a niche in the market and develop a one-of-a-kind product, I'd have it made. I could be a doctor just for the fun of it. I could have the flexibility to stay at home with my kids if I wanted to, or travel the world whenever I wanted to, and live it up like the four-hour-work-week fraternity standard.

Well, y'all, I quickly discovered that online businesses are like anything else in life. They take time and effort, and there is no such thing as an overnight success. I tried a food blog for a few months; I got the expensive camera and lighting equipment and everything. I realized quickly that the only part of food blogging I enjoyed was cooking. The whole recipe development, staging, and prepping of food was not my jam. Dropped that. Then, I started a lifestyle blog for women in medicine. This time, I got a fancy-pants designer and shelled out a couple thousand to have a fabulous website, and it really was a beautiful design. Except, I didn't post a single thing. Ever. (Oh dear, the thousands I have sunk into different "business ideas." Some women spend money on clothes and shoes. Apparently, I spend money on online businesses. Really, it's quite comical. If only I had the same gumption for reading medical journals.)

After residency, I got serious for once. I finally had more depth and understanding of not only my expertise but also the realm of online businesses. I created courses geared toward helping women overcome postpartum depression and anxiety. I was invited to speak on several podcasts, I wrote several guest blog posts, and I continued to grow my community of like-minded women. But I still felt like I was holding back. I was pigeon-holing myself into arenas that were safe for me. I know medicine. I know psychiatry. I know women. I'm good at my job. I get paid a lot of money to do my craft.

That's the thing with achievements. When we have excellence in something, we can easily be blinded to the true desires of our heart. Being good, great, or excellent at something does not mean that it is what we are meant to do. For me, I had been playing it safe. While I still loved being a doctor, I needed a challenge. I needed to reconnect with my heart, to share my heart with the world. One thing I have learned through all of my failures is this: you can't be successful at anything without heart.

Whether it is medical school, college, a relationship, or an online business, you can't be successful without heart. Your heart is what drives you forward after failure. Your heart is what creates intimacy and trust with your partner. Your heart is what draws in followers and builds a lasting platform. There is no way on God's green Earth that my food blog or lifestyle website would ever become anything bigger than my intentions for creating it in the first place, because my intentions were based on fear and doubt, and my progress quickly stalled. What you now hold in your hands is my "F you" to fear and doubt. Time will tell if my theory holds true.

On Goals

I like goals. I thrive on goals. I also don't usually have the problem of not starting something. They say the biggest hurdle to accomplishing your goals is getting started. As the go-getter that I am, I love the thrill and high that comes from starting something new. So, for me, starting something is easy. Finishing, on the other hand, is a different story.

I reflect on the many goals lists that I have made for myself. After reading more than a hundred personal development books out there, I've tried all kinds of goal setting. While I have been very successful at turning my dreams into goals and goals into reality, I also have noticed one thing. Whenever I accomplish a goal, I don't actually feel any different from before I accomplished the goal. It happens all the time.

We set goals. We join accountability groups. We pay for individual coaching. All with one hope of changing our internal state. One of the most common forms of accountability are based around weight loss under the guise of health and fitness goals.

There's the 30-day challenges and the 12-week transformation contests. How many times have you joined an accountability group or announced your goals to your entire social media feed? My question for you is, how has that made you feel?

First of all, while accountability in and of itself can be good, many of the reasons for seeking accountability are all part of the details of life that I think we should not be engaging in the first place. For example, why do you feel the need to transform the aesthetics of your body in the first place? Or why do you feel as though you need to grow your online platform or increase your sales in your business? We often don't take the time to connect with our underlying motivations, which are often rooted in fear or insecurity.

Then, what happens when you don't accomplish your goals? If you're like many of us, the hangover of perceived failure wears you down, because no matter if you actually accomplished the goal that you set out to accomplish or not, it's never good enough. What do you feel? Shame, guilt, sadness, disappointment, frustration, inadequacy... I guarantee that you do not feel happiness, joy, or excitement after the perceived failure. What are you to do instead?

Well, let's back up to the heart of the matter. Why did you make the goal in the first place? Why did you join the accountability group at all? What were you hoping to make possible? I guarantee you that it had nothing to do with the goal itself. It had to do with how you wanted to feel.

You make a goal to lose weight, because you hope to feel better. You join the accountability group, because you want to share your victory and feel important. You want the rush of dopamine that comes when you accomplish a goal or check off an item on your to-do list, because at the end of the day, something inside is telling you that you are not worthy just as you are. Some deep part of yourself is craving more.

Please realize that there is nothing inherently wrong with goal-setting and achievements. It's just that accomplishing goals for the sake of accomplishing goals will never change anything on the inside. Goals and achievements must be a result of a response to the desires of our heart, not an effort to create passion within. If you're currently in the midst of failure or doubt, or what I like to call the "muddy middle" of achievement, honor this time. Reconnect with your heart. Check your motives. If your heart's not in it, it's not worth your time.

Our heart is not begging for more things, more accolades, more stuff. Our heart is begging to be heard. When we hear its beat and respond, we get to live in the pleasure of our purpose every day. Our heart beats strong. We just need to hear its cry.

Find Your HEART

- ♥ **Here and Now.** What current goals or achievements are you working toward?
- ♥ **Embrace Your Emotions.** What feelings arise when you imagine taking a break from your goals?
- ♥ **Analyze Your Thoughts.** What meaning have you attached to achievements and goals?
- ♥ **Reflect On Your Past.** When do you remember first putting emphasis on goal-setting and personal accomplishments?
- ♥ **Take Action.** Take a one month break from to-do lists and personal development. Hide your goals sheet. Unsubscribe from personal development emails or podcasts. Celebrate all your previous successes and wins, big and small.

16
Beyond the Hearts and Hashtags

We live in an exciting world where we can connect with millions of people with the click of a button. Yet, we also feel more alone now than ever before. Research shows that the more time an individual spends on social media, the more likely they are to experience depression and anxiety. Social media usage is also correlated with "contagious" mental illnesses, like eating disorders, suicidality, and self-injurious behaviors. While research doesn't differentiate between correlation and causation, we can all agree that too much social media use can lead to self-destruction. Aimlessly scrolling your newsfeed will almost never lead to positive enlightenment. More commonly, it will lead to comparison games or impulse purchases.

Now, there are some incredibly beneficial uses for social media. Outside of the obvious means of connecting to people you may otherwise never interact with, social media has been proven to enhance the benefits of antidepressants and to decrease effects of stress and trauma disorders after traumatic events. Social media also serves to bring a voice to vulnerable populations or those in marginalized roles. Plus, it's a great modality for severely socially anxious or pathologically introverted individuals whereby traditional means of connection are not feasible.

You can't see someone's heart through social media newsfeeds. Although social media platforms have added live streaming and stories, there are still countless loopholes. Every day, thousands of new apps and software systems are being created with the intention of making the "real life" look picture-perfect. It's like the magazine model who is wearing gallons of hair gel to make her hair look "natural" or the actress who wears pounds of makeup just to look like she isn't wearing any makeup at all. The same is true for social media. You have a buffet of options at your fingertips. You can adjust lighting, colors, sound quality, clips, and music to conform to the image you want to portray. You can even make "live" videos that are not actually broadcast live.

Not to mention the amount of engineering that goes into what actually shows up in your news feed, curated to such specification as to keep you on the platform longer. Facebook wants you to go into a black hole and never leave Facebook. Instagram wants you to have never-ending scrolling and story-watching. None of us are immune. We all face this problem. And it will continue to be a problem for as long as social media remains an integral part of our lives.

Stop Comparing

Comparison is the thief of joy. Comparing yourself to someone else is the fastest way to disconnect with yourself and begin living from a disheartened place. Comparison never leads to joy or happiness. It always ends in jealousy, bitterness, anger, or resentment. Of course, you know that, or else you wouldn't be reading this book.

So, what do you do about it? First, become aware. Sometimes people just have this vague sense of emptiness when they get off social media. You go on social media to check and see how many likes the latest picture of your baby got (I know you do). Before you know it, you've entered the black hole of social media. Clicking on links, following ads, scrolling articles, sharing blog posts, and then returning to your own profile (did I get anymore likes?). You can quickly and easily lose yourself without realizing what led you down the black hole in the first place.

Beyond the what, you need to assess the who. Who is triggering you? It's easy to unfollow, unfriend, or unsubscribe. I recommend you clean up your social media feed to promote a more encouraging environment for you. What's more important though is this: why is this bothering you in the first place? When you see someone who is *doing* what you want to be doing or who *has* what you want to have, stop and reflect.

Do you even want that thing in the first place? As in, before you saw her post, would it have even crossed your mind that this was something that you wanted or needed? I feel this way commonly when I see cute arts and crafts, DIY projects, or upcycled furniture. I really love engaging my creative side, but I do not have the artist gene. I have tried (and failed) too many projects to name. I can doodle, color, and cut in a straight line, but drawing, designing, painting, sewing, knitting, and crafting are no longer worth my energy. The key is to uncover your own areas of weakness and then give yourself some grace. We cannot do it all.

You don't need to stop creating though. I'm all about creative expression. While I am limited in the arts and crafts department, I now find my creative release in other artistic expressions: cooking, baking, dancing, singing, listening to music, writing, or dreaming. And every so often, I still try my hand at the latest Pinterest trend. The difference now is, I'm more than okay with failure.

Escape the Virtual Reality

I was never very good at video games when I was a kid. A lack of spatial reasoning, they call it. I also wasn't allowed to have Nintendo as a child either (that may have something to do with it). Still, I remember trying to navigate a colonoscopy scope in medical school. For a while, I thought I wanted to specialize in gastroenterology, so I interned with a gastroenterologist for a summer. He allowed me to experiment with the scope. They use scopes to perform endoscopies and colonoscopies. It's basically just what it sounds like: a long tube with a small camera on the end and a couple of switches on the handle to navigate the camera and the forceps that pinch the lining of the gut to remove polyps or pathology samples.

I never got the hang of it. You have to watch a television screen and guide your scope based on what you see on this small screen. I would run into the gut wall, miss a curve in the small intestine, not puncture the epithelium in the right location. Basically, I was inept. My supervisor was kind and encouraging, but even he saw that I had a huge handicap when it came to these sorts of things. For the record, I had difficulty with the laparoscopic surgery camera for this very same reason.

Social media is not unlike an endoscopy. We are trying to maneuver through an organ of life by what we see on a screen, not what we can palpate with our hands, except that the world we see on social media is not a living, breathing human being with inflammatory bowel disease. It's a superficial, online, marketer-filled, troll-ridden world. Like directing a scope, it's hard to tell what's up from down, in from out, or left from right. And much like in gastroenterology, you come across a lot of sh*t.

Look Deeper

What you see is not what you get. We must accept that even live videos are not real life and that even a heartfelt blog post may not actually be from the heart. We all have an agenda these days, myself included. Whether that is an agenda of sharing pictures with your family or saving lives with your message is beside the point. The sheer fact of being seen on social media is a fallacy. It's ironic that women would say they connect with friends more on social media than in real life. I'm not knocking you by any means; to be a busy working mom who lives far from family without close friends nearby can be lonely. Social media is a nice stand-in for our heart's desire for connection.

No matter how seemingly transparent someone is online, it is still not real life. It is literally five seconds of a 24-hour period, maybe a 60-second video clip. If someone is a normal human being, they are not showing the worst sides of themselves. You do not see them fighting with their husbands or disciplining their toddlers. You do not see their messy playrooms or dirty dishes. And you definitely don't see their inner tears, hurts, struggles, and doubts.

I'm not saying that everyone should now go bearing their souls and showing their dark skeletons on social media. In fact, I think these kinds of overshares are mostly triggering to the same people you assume may be served. In effect, sharing this kind of depressing content frequently is largely self-serving and self-gratifying. All I ask is this: please stop comparing your daily life to another woman's highlight reel.

Online Marketing

Everyone is selling to us these days. In a matter of seconds of being online, you will face an advertisement or promoted post or sponsored story. You cannot escape the fact that our brains will view millions of advertisements a day. Not to mention the message from these ads is usually "you're not good enough" in one way, shape, or form. It's no wonder why we are so miserable. But I digress.

Think critically. Do not bring on your own troubles. Let's face it, online marketing unfortunately makes money by preying on vulnerable women. They convince us that we have a problem when we don't and show us that they have a solution to that problem. Before we know it, we are swimming in emails of forgotten downloads. We invest in expensive programs promising to transform some seemingly benign element of our lives.

The more I observe the online marketing space in general, the more I see a strikingly similar analogy to direct marketing pyramid schemes. Most of the people with "social proof" determined by popularity and number of likes were some of the founding members of a given platform. No matter how consistent you are or how unique you are now, you will likely never be as popular as someone who started her online business 10 years ago. This brings me to my next point.

Likes and Followers

Stop determining your self-worth by the number of likes, shares, downloads, or followers you have. I thought we left the "in" crowd back in high school, but unfortunately we are all still privy to the ongoing need to be included.

Last year, I noticed a friend of mine had two social media accounts. She had barely posted on one of the accounts, so I asked her about it. She proceeded to mention that she had started a side hobby of interior design and used her secondary Instagram profile to post about her side hobby. She seemed embarrassed, so she continued on to explain that she did not have time for her hobby much and had new priorities in this season of her life. We discussed for a while about whether she should just merge the two accounts or keep up her side hobby. Her final comment stuck with me. She said, "Stefani, sometimes, you just want a Like. Am I right?"

She is right. And she's not alone. As with every other manufactured device on social media, the sheer notifications of likes and followers create a state similar to addiction. Yes, we become addicted to seeing more likes and followers, but what we really want more than the instantaneous dopamine surge is the lasting feeling of belonging and validation. We now drink our daily cup of self-worth in units of likes and follows. We assume that because our latest picture, meme, or goofy cat video is receiving loads of traffic that we are more valuable to society.

Full disclosure here: this is something I personally work on every day. I'm aware that image is important, and I always want to represent myself and my brand with style and grace. I also know what goes into a professional photo shoot. After expertly applied makeup with fake eyelashes and perfect contouring, you then spend several hours with the help of a professional photographer and ideal lighting, weather, and background. With coaching, your body can be positioned into the best shapes and angles that accentuate your figure. Then, there is further enhancement to the photos prior to releasing print rights of the photographs. That's just for personal brand photography. Just think of what goes into commercial and print images.

While it is a true delight to be all dolled up and to be treated to a professional photography session, we must be able to see past it. Just because someone's photos are picturesque does not mean her life is picture perfect. Enjoy the beautiful photos but also don't be afraid to share photos that are not entirely perfect. Be true to who you are, unabashedly. And when viewing another's seemingly perfect feed, just keep in mind that no one is perfect.

Find Your HEART

- 💜 **Here and Now.** What thoughts arise as you scroll social media or view certain profiles?
- 💜 **Embrace Your Emotions.** What feelings or emotions arise?
- 💜 **Analyze Your Thoughts.** What meaning do you attach to these thoughts and feelings?
- 💜 **Reflect On Your Past.** When do you remember feeling this way before in the past?
- 💜 **Take Action.** Social Media Detox. Unfriend, unfollow, hide, unsubscribe, or delete any accounts that bring you down.

Part 4

Live from Your Heart

A life wholly lived is a life wholly loved
From God above, our purpose renews
To live and love, wholly you
Be you and you, for God above
Live from the heart, awaken within

A life wholly lived, a life wholly loved
From God above, our passion prevails
To have and hold, wholly you
Be you and you, for you alone
Live out your heart, shine outward

A life wholly lived, a life wholly loved
From God above, our plan unfolds
To be and let be, wholly you
Be you and you, for all around
Live beyond the heart, touch afar

-Stefani Reinold

17
Find the Beat of Your HEART

I remember the first time I heard my daughter's heartbeat. I was pregnant for the first time. My husband had to work, but my mom had driven down to go to my first ultrasound appointment with me. I was already feeling anxious about knowing my due date. I was in my fourth and final year of medical school, and I was hoping that I would be able to have my baby without taking time off of school, and still be able to start residency on time next summer. I approached motherhood like many things in my life: plan, work, execute. Clearly, I was living in my thoughts.

After waiting almost 30 minutes, I got all of my initial lab draws and was taken back to the exam room to receive my very first ultrasound, which a delightful nurse midwife performed. I will never forget that moment. The midwife was searching for the little being, a process that took only seconds but felt like agony for this first-time mom. Then, in a blink, she found the tiny embryo staring from the screen. I saw the little flicker of a heartbeat on this impossibly small being, and I heard music to my ears. *Pa–Pa–Pa–Pa-Pa–Pa.* It was so quick. Was this normal? Yes, this was normal. Before I could even think, tears began welling in my eyes. And my mom's too. There was a baby living inside of me. I was having a baby. While I still experienced morning sickness and fatigue like nobody's business, I was rejuvenated that day and felt at peace, and excited for my future as a mom. I couldn't wait to tell Travis.

Like hearing my daughter's heartbeat for the first time on ultrasound, finding your heartbeat in your own life is the same overflow of emotions. In order to live fully from the bottom of your heart, you first have to find your heartbeat. Most women I have helped find their own heartbeat are so overcome with emotions that they cry. These are tears of pure joy. They are the tears of a woman who has been striving and searching her whole life to finally drop into the bottom of herself, to feel and know that she will be okay, and more than that, she now knows the way back. When we can find our heartbeat once, we can continue to find it again and again, no matter our circumstances or the situation at hand.

Your heartbeat is within you. You haven't lost it, like so many women think. It's just been covered up with a ton of gunk and grime. If you've done the work thus far, you're there. Don't worry if it's different from the next girl. It's yours. Your heart is unique to you. Recognizing those moments can be quite challenging. We habitually cover up the moments, either because we are uncomfortable with the feeling or we have so many negative associations with them.

Envision a time when you felt your heart. I don't like using the word happy, because it's a fleeting emotion, but if it helps you to think of the "happiest day of your life," you can think about it that way. Some common examples include: the day you got engaged or married, had your baby, started or finished a new project, or had a great holiday experience. Don't overthink this. Finding your heartbeat is not some over-the-top, on-top-of-the-world feeling. It is a moment where you feel completely connected and alive, as if nothing else matters.

186

Describe that time in your life. What were you doing? Who were you with? How did you feel about yourself? Where were you? What were details of your life at the time?

Now, review the last 24 hours of your life. If necessary, you may need to expand it to a few days, a week, or even a month. What moments or memories immediately stand out to you? Why did these feelings stand out to you? Reflect on any feelings that arise. Anger. Joy. Peace. Stress. Overwhelmed. Lighthearted. Love.

Can you find any moments in the last day or week when you felt your heart?

To live from the heart is to be ready for anything, to reach a place where you can feel any feeling, let it rush over you. Like waves beating over the rocks, you must be a rock that is open and willing to take a beating now and again, knowing that it will pass. You will get through it.

This shall too pass.

In Your Element

Before I started my first semester at Baylor University, I attended a Baylor Line Camp. Line Camps are an opportunity for fellow incoming students to meet others in a close-knit, intimate setting. We had each taken the StrengthsFinder test and part of our retreat was to discuss our various strengths and how we could embrace them and utilize them in college. I've gone on to take the test a few times in my life, and one of my top strengths is always Activator. People with the Activator strength are good initiators and feel best when starting new things. You easily begin new projects, conversations, or what-have-you. You feel energized by the newness of things. (Yep, definitely me.)

One of my Line Camp counselors, Haley, was amazing. She was one of those women you meet and you can feel the warmth of her soul just by being in her presence. By earthly standards, she was not exceptionally pretty, but in one short conversation, you couldn't help but think, *Wow, she has a beautiful soul.* That feeling she gave me when I was talking to her cannot be put into words. If I tried, I would surely not do it justice.

I also met other truly amazing people at this camp. Some are still dear friends to this day. I remember very little about the nuts and bolts of the camp, but I do remember it was in a cute cabin west of Fort Worth. We ate three meals a day, had quiet time in the morning, did some group activities together, and talked for hours with new friends who I met on the car ride there. Outside of going over our StrengthsFinder results, I don't remember many details about the camp.

What I do remember is how I *felt* at the camp. When I look back on my life, there are maybe 10 or so isolated events where I felt fully "in my element," or what I now call living from the heart. This was one of those times. I was not insecure. I did not doubt. I was just being me around other people who were being them. I felt alive and full of life at the same time.

When the academic year started, it was nice to have some friends in a busy place. Frankly, I lost touch with many of my fellow Line Campers though. It is what it is. We went on to join different clubs, we lived in different dorms, we joined different sororities and fraternities, we chose different majors. Sometime later I ran into Haley on campus. I had recently formed a very large pre-med organization on campus, and we had one of our first meetings with a big speaker. She asked me how it went. I replied, "Good!" with an anxious smile. She retorted, "Were you in your element?" My face loosened. My body relaxed. I thought about it a moment. I finally said with a genuine smile, "Yes."

I didn't know it at the time, but that experience has led to some of my greatest revelations in my adult life. I know that I thrive in small group, camp-like, retreat experiences. I'd rather go deep with a few people than be superficial with the masses. I also sincerely love public speaking. I am energized by hearing people's stories. I wish I could say that after my brief moment of clarity I went on to live fully "in my element" all the time, only seeking opportunities that allowed me to be living from the heart, but unfortunately, that's just not reality. It would take me some 10+ years later to fully realize my potential, to reconnect with my truest self, and to live from the bottom of my heart.

Making Space

I wish I could tell you that, once you find your heartbeat, you will gallantly ride along on your white horse in the meadows of heart-centered living and never have a care in the world. Life doesn't work that way. You will get knocked down. You will fail. You will live in your head. You will avoid your emotions. You will fall for some superficial detail of life and let it consume you for more days than you care to admit.

I began my own journey back to my heart about five years ago. I say "back to," because I never lost myself. I momentarily strayed further from my center, but I have always been me. And even in my less-than-genuine moments of my life, I was still me. I am the consummation of all the broken, partitioned, and whole pieces of my past. These days, I feel truly purposeful and overwhelmingly present. I live my life with intention, so that even when I choose to do things that are not my utmost passion, I do them with intention. I have a clear vision for my life, but I am open for the crazy whirlwind that comes at me. I no longer let the details of life consume me.

I am also 100% human. I am a full-time working mother of two with little to no support system around me, a two-hour flight away from the closest family. And I still allow distractions to consume me at times. In the writing of this book, I took a five-day hiatus from writing to read a four-part romance novel series. It became an obsession. I not only had to finish the first book, but then I had to finish every single book in the series. It took me a few days to figure out what I was doing. I had gotten out of my normal workout routine, avoided spending quality time with my children and husband, and even neglected my personal hygiene for a couple of days, all so I could finish a stupid book series. (It was very enjoyable, I'll admit. *London Lovers* series by Amy Daws).

When I finally came around, I shook myself up. I came to the realization that I was avoiding finishing this book. I had several fears racing through my mind. *What if no one reads it? What if nobody likes it? What if people judge me? What if? What if?* You can let your fears consume you into a tailspin of anxiety, but the only way to bring yourself out of a situation like that is to make space for exactly what you are experiencing.

Make space for the fears. I wrote down all of my fears that I had in publishing this book. I shared some of the fears with my husband, who is my best friend and confidante. Afterward, I tore up my fears. I then wrote my biggest fantasies. I set aside time in my schedule to dream. Literally. I scheduled 30 minutes a day in my last week of writing this book so that I could just dream, no concrete vision planning, just time to truly dream. Let your mind go wild.

Reign Yourself In

After you regularly make space for yourself, you must become accustomed to reigning yourself in. This takes time, practice, and a lot of patience with yourself. Find your weak points. In my example, reading other books was my way of avoiding my own writing. This paradox is common. From my experience, your coping strategy is often the exact opposite of what you want to do. For instance, people working on improving their relationships choose to isolate themselves socially and do more tasks by themselves. Others who are trying to follow a budget and save money end up spending more money on others rather than themselves. Those who are trying to improve their health obsess over the details of their diets and workout plans, instead of actually spending time moving their bodies or experimenting with new recipes.

We each have our own special weaknesses. I know from several years of being a control freak that the more I plan, the more I am avoiding accomplishing tasks at hand. Now, I choose to plan as little as possible. Though, please don't take this as advice to you. You must come to find your own vice. What is holding you back from feeling your heartbeat? How do you stop living for the details and start reigning yourself in?

Mind you, coping skills can be incredibly therapeutic. I'm only suggesting that when you allow a coping skill to overcompensate for other areas of your life, you may need to stop and take a step back. Investigate the heart of the matter, the heart of *you*. Only then will you be able to feel your heartbeat.

Find Your HEART

- ♥ **Here and Now.** How many moments in your life do you currently feel in your element?
- ♥ **Embrace Your Emotions.** What feelings or physical sensations arise when you are living in your element?
- ♥ **Analyze Your Thoughts.** Why do you feel that these specific moments or activities made you feel in your element?
- ♥ **Reflect On Your Past.** When do you first remember feeling this way?
- ♥ **Take Action.** What small action can you take today to feel in your element?

18
Mothering with Heart

There is no change more paramount in all your life as there is when you become a mother. The struggle to conform to and abide by the cultural norms and standards is real. It may take several years in the trenches of motherhood, but no mother is immune to the identity crisis that coexists with the birth of your baby.

I'm not sure why I had a baby. Many women aren't. I mean, I ask hundreds of women why they had a baby, and they usually just say, "Well, I always imagined being a mother." It's programmed deep within us. This is a good thing. I mean, we wouldn't continue the human race unless we had babies. But still, I would hope that some women had some deeper purpose for having babies. Nope. Also, we like to think that the love expands so much from your marriage that you just have to bring another life into this world. It's oftentimes why even women who don't have babies will have a pet (or several pets). We just can't handle the overwhelming emotions within us, so we must displace some of those feelings onto another living being. And so the plight of motherhood goes. We often continue projecting our feelings onto others. Then, we can't tell where we end and our children begin.

We are vulnerable to attack on all fronts. When we have babies, it's as if we taped a red, flashing light to our bellies that reads "touch me." For me, honestly, it never bothered me. I crave physical touch, and I guess I liked the attention. Nonetheless, it is extremely intrusive and odd that we can be subjected to touch so often. And, of course, everyone's first question when you're pregnant is "How's it going? You're glowing. You're so cute. I love baby bumps." And then within seconds of having the baby, it shifts to "Oh, she's so beautiful. Can I hold her? So little. How precious." This leaves you feeling like chopped liver over here in the corner. Not to mention, your, umm, hygiene is less-than-normal. I mean, I had C-sections that made me feel like Frankenstein who was just sewed up and spit out with an ever bloated and expanding belly. I thought, *I already had the kid, why does my belly still feel like I'm carrying a child?* It takes time, that's what everyone says. It takes time to get your sex drive back. It takes time to get used to things. It takes time to find your new normal. It takes time to get a groove. How much time? Precisely six weeks, according to the medical community.

"All right, you're good to go," was what my OB told me at six weeks. Good to go where? What do you mean? I'm not sleeping. Sex is painful. I lactate when I orgasm. And I've ruined at least two nice blouses already because I've leaked through my nursing pads. And I feel I'll be in maternity pants for the rest of my life.

And now, onto the sex thing itself. Nothing extinguishes a woman in heat more than a baby. Seriously, it's like they're programmed with a switch to cry every single time my husband and I would just about be ready to get it on.

Then, my husband would pull the "oh just let her cry, she'll be fine." Um, yeah try that one on for size. There's no way I could get in the mood listening to my baby cry in the background. How's that for ambiance? For the record, I think the lovemaking thing only gets worse as the kids get older. Now they're mobile, and they definitely don't understand the need for personal space, unless it's while you're pooping. Nope, just kidding, not even then. (Note to self: any future house I buy will have a lock on the master bedroom.)

All this to say: being yourself as a new mother is next to impossible. The expectations for moms in particular are at an all-time ridiculous level. It used to be that to be a good wife meant having dinner ready, caring for the children while your husband worked, and making a pie or two for new neighbors. Then, we had to keep up the home and provide financially for our families. Our parents' generation faced the rise of working women, where they not only had to maintain the home but also had to manage a full-time job.

Now in our generation, it is not enough to be working with children. We also add starting a side hustle, volunteering for PTA, planning Pinterest-worthy birthday parties, doing daily arts and crafts projects for the kids, living the four-hour-workweek, writing a bestselling book, caring for our aging parents, traveling the world to show our kids culture, all while walking around with a perpetual smile, reciting Bible verses off the cuff, breastfeeding exclusively for two years (because nothing short of that would be child abuse), preparing delicious, organic, real food meals and snacks for our kids and making sure they love it (because if they don't, it's our fault). And, of course, looking like a Victoria's Secret model while we do it. Did I catch it all? You may think I'm joking, but this is precisely the pressure we women place on ourselves, all while recovering from a pregnancy and childbirth.

A patient of mine described it best when she lamented that she, as a new mom, felt utilitarian. We are utilitarian. The rote work of motherhood inundates our minds. We go through each part of our perfectly planned out days with the only goal of making it to the next schedule of the day. We lose sight of the deeper issues until life hits us in the face.

"Excuse me, excuse me, what are you doing?" I hastened. I saw two ladies reaching through the open window into the backseat of my car where Kate was buckled in her car seat. It appeared to be an older mom with her college-aged daughter.

They were silent.

"Excuse me, get away from my daughter!" I shrieked. I entered the backseat from the other side. I quickly caught glimpse of a screaming, red-faced, three-month-old Kate, and it appeared that she blew out her diaper.

"Well, ma'am, we were just walking and saw—" the mother said.

"Thank you, thank you," I interrupted. I put up my hand to barricade the woman away from my baby. "I got it from here, thank you. I'm her *mother*."

"Well, we called the cops. We didn't know—" the daughter said. They appeared nervous. The tension between us all was tight.

"WHAT?! You called the COPS?!?!" I shrieked. I freaked out. I was going to lose my baby. How could I do this to her? I was the worst mother in the world. I was like those mothers you see on television, a bad mom, like, really bad mom. No one had ever called the cops on me. Sure, I've had my share of speeding tickets and dumb parking tickets but have never been arrested. I even managed to smoke pot legally when I studied abroad in the Netherlands.

"Well, ma'am, your daughter was screaming. It's the middle of July. We didn't see you around." Yes, she was right. I had left my baby girl in the car. Remember me telling you I had postpartum depression? Yeah, this could've been the first tipoff.

196

"I'm here now, okay? I'm here now," I reassured them. By this point, I had taken Kate out of her car seat and was cleaning her up in the backseat. I was drenched in sweat in my workout clothes. Kate's clothes were wrecked from sweat, poop, and tears. Thank God I brought the diaper bag with us.

"Where were you? We didn't see you around."

"I had just stepped into Smoothie King." I paused. Tears were beginning to well in my eyes. *I left my daughter in the car.* The realization hit me. *Who am I?* I didn't want to wake her. We had been running errands all morning. I wanted to let her rest. I remembered to put all the windows down. It was only a few minutes. I kept an eye on her the whole time.

"Okay… well… I mean…" they were struggling to find words. Clearly, they saw the desperation in my face. "The cops are still on their way. I already called them," the daughter reminded me. I saw their perplexed looks on their faces as they looked at each other and back at me. They were deciding whether or not I was one of those crazy moms who harms their child or if I had a momentary lapse in judgment. Hopefully, they'd settle on the latter.

I finished changing her diaper and searched her diaper bag for an extra onesie. "Please, just give me some grace. I screwed up okay? I'm not perfect. She's my daughter. I'm her mother. I've got her now." Always err on the side of honesty. I buttoned the last button on her onesie.

"Yeah, I know. We're not perfect either," the mother remarked, though her tone was tainted with judgment and arrogance. She may have been giving lip service to sympathy, but her face screamed, *I'm better than you.*

"Yeah, okay, thank you. I mean, I have to go now. I'm leaving." With that, I quickly buckled Kate back in her car seat and sat down in the driver's seat. I fastened my seatbelt and drove away, evading the cops in the process. My heart was beating out of my chest. I had never been so scared. Later that evening, I shared my traumatic experience with Travis. I was angry and frustrated. I was beating myself up. I'm a horrible mother. I left my baby in the car. She could've died. I could've gone to jail. I could've lost her. Child Protective Services would have gotten involved. I'm so horrible.

As I relayed the details of the day, Travis listened, taking it all in. When I had finished my wallowing, he grabbed me by the hips and pulled me close. Instead of judging or analyzing, he looked me in the eyes and said, "We all make mistakes."

I've since decided that motherhood is all about mistakes. If you are not making mistakes, you are probably doing something wrong. We all fear that we will "screw up" our kids. The more I'm entrenched in psychodynamic theories, the more I throw up my hands in surrender. I have accepted that no matter what I do, I will probably screw up my kids. Not that I don't try to avoid inflicting harm to my child, but I now understand that juvenile brains are incredibly vulnerable. No matter how hard I try, I am a fallible human and will undoubtedly say something that is taken out of context.

Instead of fearing that you will inevitably cause some baggage in your kids' life, why not instead investigate the baggage in your own life. Behind your fears almost certainly lies some unconscious insecurity of your own. While consciously trying to fill the void in your own heart, you unconsciously pass down the same baggage to your children. This is called *repetition compulsion*. It explains why similar patterns are passed from generation to generation.

For example, fathers who have anger problems likely raise sons with anger problems. Mothers with body image issues will raise daughters with body image issues. The only way to stop the cycle is to reconnect with the underlying issues driving the conscious problem in the first place, not just correcting the anger behavior, but correcting the drive that creates the anger. Our children, unfortunately, have become the catch-all of our emotion du jour. I see it all the time. Women transfer their own insecurities onto their children, or they live out their own desires through their kids. This has to stop. You are not doing yourself or your children any favors by projecting all of your own baggage onto your children.

On the flip side, your child is her own person. She has unique gifts, talents, and skills. And, as any mother of a preschooler can attest, she also has her own faults, weaknesses, and limitations. It can be challenging to be in the presence of a whining, screaming toddler. Witnessing a temper tantrum riles up feelings of inadequacy, anger, frustration, and even worthlessness in ourselves. To combat the discomfort within ourselves, we lash out in anger toward our helpless toddler. When we can't control our child's reaction, we feel a sense of failure and unworthiness. Remove your sense of self-worth from your child. Stop expecting perfection from them, and stop trying to control how they should or should not react to a given circumstance. We can no more control how our children act than we can control the weather.

There is no perfect plan that will lead to perfect children and no one perfect system that will bring about the desired outcome in motherhood. Donald W. Winnicott, famous pediatrician and psychoanalyst, coined the term "good enough mothering." Good enough mothering is the premise that with basic, normal, good-natured parenting, kids will have all they need to mature into healthy, well-adjusted adults. Granted, there was no such thing as Pinterest in Winnicott's day, but his premise still remains. There is no such thing as perfection. There is no such thing as good. Only good enough. And you, mama, are good enough.

Find Your *HEART*

- ♥ **Here and Now.** Replay a recent emotionally charged scene with your child.
- ♥ **Embrace Your Emotions.** What emotions or physical sensations arise?
- ♥ **Analyze Your Thoughts.** What about the situation triggered these particular emotions? What is the underlying message?
- ♥ **Reflect On Your Past.** How do you imagine your relationship with your own mother or experiences from your childhood could be playing a role in this situation?
- ♥ **Take Action.** Find a community of likeminded moms.

19
When You Can't HEAR your HEART

On January 31, 2015, I awoke in the middle of the night to stabbing pelvic pain. *Owe… Owe. Owe. Owe… Omg, what is wrong with me?* I had been spotting for the last day but hadn't thought much of it. I spotted when I was pregnant with Kate. The doctors called it "implantation bleeding" at the time. I assumed this was the same, though I was quite a few weeks further along this time. *The embryo should've implanted already*, I thought to myself.

Then, I felt it. Gush… I was now lying in a small pool of blood that was drenching the sheets. *Owe…* another stabbing pelvic pain. I ran to the bathroom trickling blood along the way. I sat down on the toilet. *Owe, owe, owe….* I was now barreling over in pain. *Is this what a contraction feels like?* I thought. I had experienced minimal labor with Kate before having a C-section because she was breech. *Wait… what am I saying? Contractions… Contractions could only mean one thing.*

I stumbled over to Travis sleeping soundly in bed. "Baby…" I was holding back tears already. I knew what was happening. "Travis... please wake up..." He was groggy, barely in a daze. I couldn't hold this back anymore. "Travis... I... I..." I could barely speak. My throat was sore from restraining my cries. I had to tell him. He needed to know. He'll know what to do. He always does.

"Yeah?" he mumbled half in a daze.

"Travis, I need you." My voice was stern. Silent tears began flowing out of my eyes. Travis looked up. It was dark in our bedroom, but he must have felt my weakness. I'm not one to wake him up in the middle of the night.

"Oh no, what's wrong?" He looked concerned. He knew something was wrong.

"I... I... Travis, I think I'm having a miscarriage," I blurted out before I collapsed on the bed in his arms. He was now wide awake. He didn't say anything. He didn't have to. The tears spilling out of his eyes said it all. (I've only seen my husband cry three times in my life. First, when he left me for his deployment to Iraq. Second, at a memorial for his West Point roommate who was killed in action. Third, when I had a miscarriage. There may have been a fourth time during *Million Dollar Baby*, but you didn't hear that from me.)

A few days later, I was sitting at the OB office. This was supposed to be my first obstetrics appointment for this pregnancy. It was the clinic's routine to get a transvaginal ultrasound at your first appointment to date your pregnancy accurately. Then you would meet with the doctor. I was lying down in stirrups waiting for the ultrasound technician to discover what I already knew. The pregnancy was no longer viable.

"Well, this confirms it," she said matter-of-fact. "You see here, it appears as though you have expelled the remnants completely," she explained as she turned the ultrasound screen toward me and Travis, who was sitting patiently next to me, holding my hand. Expelled... It sounds like some poison that your body must remove in order to protect you. This didn't feel like protection. This felt like betrayal. My body betrayed me. I could feel the tears welling up inside of me again. "All right, you can sit up now. I will now get the doctor," she instructed.

I was very thankful for her calm demeanor. In the moment, when my mind was racing and my hormonal emotions were about to fly off the handle, I don't think I could've handled coddling or affection from my ultrasound technician. After she walked out, the tears came flowing. I couldn't hold them back.

A few minutes later, the doctor walked in. Normally a to-the-point, surgeon-like woman, she was silent. Her face had the look of sorrow and sadness. In one expression, I felt completely understood. *Maybe she's had a miscarriage herself,* I thought. Karen Kleiman, licensed clinical social worker, founder and executive director of The Postpartum Stress Center, and author of *This Isn't What I Expected,* calls this "the art of holding," a therapeutic technique whereby you create a safe, open space of holding painful feelings. (For the record, most doctors, and humans in general, are pretty poor at this. We deflect painful feelings and immediately jump in to fix a problem.) After what felt like eons of time between us, she finally spoke.

"I'm sorry," she let out. She walked closer to me. I was still crying, but the sobs had died down to small trickles down my cheeks. She then proceeded to offer medical knowledge regarding my situation (I wouldn't need a D&C but I would need to take serial pregnancy tests to make sure my HCG levels continued to drop), some counseling for the future (wait until after my next period before we begin trying to conceive again), and encouragement (miscarriages are extremely common and one miscarriage doesn't usually increase risk for future infertility). While the entire visit was cathartic, I left the office utterly exhausted.

Travis and I had been trying to get pregnant with a second baby for several months. I was not only suffering from secondary infertility, but now, I felt officially doomed. While

I was incredibly blessed with a healthy baby girl, I desperately wanted another baby. Plus, any kind of loss is a hard pill to swallow. Anyone who has experienced a miscarriage can attest, it's not necessarily the loss of life that is heart-wrenching, but it's everything you had built up in that potential life. Travis and I had already started talking about boy names and envisioned life as a family of four. I dreamed of how I could design a cute nursery within our oversized master bedroom.

It's also the silence that ensues. I can think of no other moment when I have felt more alone in the world. No one talks about moments like this, moments of loss, death, suffering. Having already experienced postpartum depression, I was more open to receiving support after my miscarriage. When I did share my story, I realized that I was hardly alone. Multitudes of women shared with me their own stories of loss and infertility.

Lastly, I wanted to atone for my perceived failures in my role as mother to Kate. I thought, *This time I'll get maternity photos, I won't drink caffeine, I'll eat all organic throughout my pregnancy, I'll have a vaginal delivery, and I'll breastfeed exclusively. I'll read to him more, I'll be present, and I'll set up his college fund immediately. I'll be better. I'll do better.* Somewhere in my distorted thinking, I still treated motherhood as another thing at which I could possibly be perfect. There is no perfect motherhood. There is no perfect birth. There is no perfect mother.

Forrest Gump had it right when he said, "Sh*t happens." There are times in life when you fall flat on your face. No amount of processing, or feeling your feelings, or reconnecting to childhood hurts will help you through the moments when you are so overcome with grief that you physically feel ill. Bankruptcy, divorce, death of a loved one, severe mental illness, national tragedy, natural disaster, loss of your job, foreclosure, or even an abrupt move can all spur the heart to close off and sink deeper into a pit. For anyone who has been through these severe trials, you know the all-consuming heartache well. It's like the large pit of forgotten memories in *Inside Out*. You have not only lost memories but have lost hope out of this painful experience. In a desperate effort to escape the hollowness you feel, you quickly revert to a former self.

After my miscarriage, my self-improvement obsessions took on a whole new level. I began restricting my calories more in an effort to change my body. I continued my online business crusades. I obsessed over my future and my career trajectory. I nagged my husband and picked petty fights. I slipped back into old habits of external aggrandizement and self-induced misery rather than processing my pain and working through the present issues.

I see it all the time. Women are bouncing along. They're challenging their thoughts, feeling their feelings, processing their past. They're improving relationships with others in the process and heart-centered living has become the norm. Then, life happens. But it's not a life you want. It's not a reality you want to face. And in an instant, all of your hard work of unpacking yourself seems to unravel in front of your eyes. You feel like the bouquet of your heart has now shattered to a thousand rose petals scattered on the beach. As you try to pick them up, the waves continue to crash harder and harder.

I won't tell you that the way out of your pain is to feel your feelings or meditate or think your way to peace. I have treated enough patients and have lived long enough to know that to utilize these techniques requires a high level of capacity, something you are sorely lacking in traumatic circumstances. When you cannot HEAR your heart, all you can do is take action. And this is the one time in this book where I encourage you to act first and think later.

The tips below are a list of actions that I created for myself to survive painful moments. I encourage you to create your own action plan. And I hope that you will create a list of actions prior to actually needing them. When you are in those low moments, you are not in the frame of mind to prioritize self-care. These tips are beyond the obvious, more mainstream acts of self-care like a good night's sleep, bubble baths, massages, and pedicures. I wanted to provide you with unique and nurturing tools that will help you overcome your pain.

- **Pray about it.** As a woman of faith, prayer has been a powerful force in my life. It has taken me years to see that God has always answered my prayers. The solutions rarely came at the times when I wanted them, but answers always came. My steadfastness in prayer held me up in my weakest of moments.

- **Hug someone you love.** In the heat of tragedy, the most important thing your heart longs for is security. The act of touch brings security through intimacy. Prolonged touch secretes oxytocin, the feel-good hormone. After finding out about my miscarriage, a dear coworker welcomed me back to work with the most all-consuming hug that lasted for at least 30 seconds. It was the most healing experience. Hugging your husband, your best friend, or your babies feeds your need for what experts call "skin hunger."

- **Ground yourself.** Grounding yourself means to assess the here and now. Connect with all five senses. Physically look around you. What do you see? Close your eyes. What do you hear? What do you smell? Lick your lips. Are there any tastes lingering on your tongue? Think about touch. What are you physically in contact with right now? What other physical manifestations arise from your body?

- **Ensure your basic needs are met**. It's easy to overlook basic needs of food, shelter, or clothing in a time of catastrophe. If you cannot cook a warm meal for yourself, enlist or accept the help of others. Find a safe shelter, both in the literal sense of a house that you feel comfortable in, and the figurative sense of finding community or family that makes you feel safe. Wear clothing that makes you feel good and brings you joy. For some, this is yoga pants and a t-shirt. For others, this is a flowy sundress or jeans and a sweatshirt. Find comfort in caring for your basic needs.

💜 **Return to your home base.** One of the first things we learn as little children is attachment, and one of the tenets of attachment theory is to have a safe and secure home base. For many of us, this is natural. When bad things happen, we want to return to our home. Whether this is the geographic location where you grew up or not is up to you. I'm giving you permission to return home. In person. For real. Right now. If this means getting on a plane or driving across country, so be it. Plan the trip. I promise you'll thank me later.

💜 **Connect with nature.** Nature is grounding. Escaping the hustle and bustle of our daily lives can go a long way toward healing. Take a hike. Go to the beach. Even a walk around the block. Use all of your senses to soak in your environment and ground yourself to the present moment.

💜 **Handwrite a letter.** Handwriting not only activates the concentration and planning centers of the brain, but it also crosses right and left-brain circuits. When you're a mud puddle of thoughts (left brain) and emotions (right brain), it's natural to feel scattered. Writing unifies the mental chaos. Write a letter to encourage yourself, or write a letter to someone or something that hurt you. Or write a letter to a loved one thanking them for getting you through a hard time. It's up to you whether you do anything with the letter or not.

♥ **Stop consuming**. On a daily basis, we are inundated with millions of messages, advertisements, and knowledge. Some, if not most, of the information we receive is entirely unhelpful, especially in times of catastrophe. Take a break from consumption (this book excluded of course). Stop consuming facts, extra knowledge, ongoing stimulation, and more information.

♥ **Delete the noise**. Along the same lines of consumption, step away from the noise in your life, both literally and figuratively. There are times in my life when my house seems like I'm living in the middle of a tornado of whines, screams, and chaos. This same noise presents itself in a myriad of situations, at work or at home. Remove yourself from these circumstances as frequently as necessary.

♥ **Smell something pleasant**. The sense of smell is our most archaic sense. Smelling something pleasant or comforting can connect us to nostalgic memories or simpler times. For me, the smell of homemade bread or crockpot chili just screams home to me. I've also been known to splash on some Jessica Simpson *Fancy* perfume to remember the early days of my courtship with Travis. Or smell something that just calms your senses, like eucalyptus or lavender.

♥ **Step away from conflict**. As much as you'd like to engage in social justice or take a stand for something important, you are not in the frame of reference to act sensibly now. If you face conflict at this time, step away. Although counterintuitive, know that stepping away is an act of bravery.

♥ **Make a list of people you trust**. In the height of chaos, we lose sight of what and who we can believe in. Forming a tangible representation of those you trust and believe in is critical. Don't be ashamed if the only person on your list right now is God, your spouse, or your mom. When life dropkicks you to the curb, just one person is enough to help you get back up.

❤ **Listen to classical music.** Like handwriting, classical music activates bilateral neuronal processes in the brain. Music therapists often will use classical music as a means of soothing terminally ill patients. It's even used in some neonatal intensive care units to help in the healing and comforting of premature babies. For an added bonus, write while listening to classical music. You'll enter a state of flow faster and with more ease, and your writing may reveal some deeper conflicts that this painful experience is bringing to light.

❤ **Find the truth.** You will be inundated with opinions or commentary. No matter what the situation, someone will give you their advice. I can't tell you to ignore the ambiguity, because that would be to stop existing. I am telling you to look beneath the surface. Behind every joke, sarcastic comment, piece of advice, or opinion is a truth. What is the emotion behind the opinion? What is the motive? What is the heart of the message?

❤ **Talk it out.** You are experiencing complex and confusing emotions right now. Professional therapy can help you process the myriad of emotions. A good therapist can also be an advocate for you with your loved ones. I personally wish I had sought professional therapy a decade before I did. I would've spared my heart a whirlwind of damage.

In the heart of suffering, it is natural to want to be a victim, to want to escape. Fight this inclination. Muster the courage to stay with your feelings as much as you can. Some days, this may be five seconds; other days, it may be five hours. Avoid the deflection toward others. Your trial is not someone's fault. It's not a punishment for wrongdoing or atonement for sins. There is only one way out of pain, and it is through it. Keep reminding yourself that this shall too pass. Because it will. It really will.

Find Your HEART

Sometimes it isn't reasonable to embrace your thoughts and emotions. Sometimes you just need to take action.

- ♥ **Take Action.** Review the list in the chapter. Create your own emergency action plan of concrete things you can do when you are faced with a very painful experience.

20
Managing Our Hearts Around Others

Woman was created to be a responder. As such, we are highly vulnerable to the environment, meaning the people, places, and things surrounding us. If one or all of those entities is off, we naturally will be affected.

I cover several related but different concepts surrounding the topic of conflict in this chapter. Know upfront that this is a super heavy topic and one that could easily be an entire book unto itself. In keeping with the scope of *this* book, I want you to review these concepts with the premise that the only person you can control is yourself. Relationships are highly complex. If we as individuals are hurting to be genuine, we can only imagine how living with and engaging with others results in a symphony of dysfunction at times.

That said, I share these concepts so that you can begin to look at those with whom you are in a relationship and see a deeper perspective. Please remember, the intent is not to place blame on someone else. Rather, the goal is to reclaim the only thing within your control: yourself. As you assess your role within your relationships, you can become mindful of how your own psyche is playing out, and how you can help improve your relationships by transforming yourself.

Naturally, we women carry the burden of emotions around us. We are designed to be the caretaker, and thus, we desire to nurture those around us. We easily neglect our own needs to manage the needs of others. As such, it also becomes easy to focus on others outside of ourselves, particularly when facing strain in a relationship. It is rather easy to become the nag, the victim, or the complainer. Women also struggle with gossip more than men. We naturally want to solve other people's problems. When we are uncomfortable around someone else, we are quick to blame that other person rather than acknowledging our role. We have within our power the ability to acknowledge and manage the emotional burden that we carry. First, we must become aware of the profound psychodynamic forces at play.

Transference and Countertransference

Let's first start with two psychodynamic vocabulary words that will help set the precedent for many interrelationship issues: transference and countertransference.

Transference is the unconscious interjection of a feeling from one person to another. In lay terms, transference refers to how you feel around someone. This likely comes up when you are around people whom you may consider "toxic." While no person is truly toxic, you may feel very negatively after interactions with certain individuals. This is due to that individual's unconscious projection of uncomfortable feelings onto you. Note that this all occurs unconsciously, meaning that these "toxic" people are likely not consciously trying to tear you down.

I remember traveling on an airplane with Kate when she was only five months old. As we were taking off, Kate was crying on my lap when a rude lady from across the aisle interjected, "Don't you need to nurse her while you take off? It helps her little ears." What the lady did not realize is that Kate had been refusing breastfeeding as of late. I had been trying to feed her a bottle, but Kate was not accepting the bottle either. We were clearly causing a scene, but literally, there was nothing more I could do.

This scenario can get extremely detailed from a psychodynamic standpoint. The simplest explanation is that the lady was feeling insecure, inadequate, or uncomfortable listening to a baby cry. This discomfort likely riled up unconscious feelings of inadequacy for her. In order to feel important, she chose to give me advice. However, what I internalized was her own unconscious feelings of inadequacy, not her well-intentioned advice. This is transference.

Transference proves that it is always the intention behind words or actions that are more important than the actual words or actions. We will unconsciously receive the feeling or motive behind an action first. (As an aside, it's also why you should not ever give out of guilt or proper etiquette. If your heart is not in it, believe me, the person receiving the gift will only feel the emotion behind the gift, not ever the gift itself.)

If transference is the unconscious projection of emotion from another person, countertransference is then our unconscious reaction to that emotion. As you can see, these concepts can get increasingly intricate. Psychoanalysts go through extensive training to become experts in transference and countertransference.

Nonetheless, it helps to explain why some "toxic" people will "get a rise out of you." It is not the person, per say, but how you unconsciously internalize or react to them. Remember that we unknowingly internalize another's unconscious pain. Then, our countertransference is how we individually react to the unconscious discomfort. For instance, imagine how you feel when you are talking to a particularly shy person or a very anxious person. More than likely, you yourself begin to feel shy or anxious. Typically, transference and countertransference are very subtle, as they are unconscious processes.

Reflect on those relationships or people in your life. What characteristics are common among these people? How do you relate to these people? The goal is to stop blaming and judging others and to instead become more mindful of the real *you*. As you notice how you feel around certain kinds of people, you can understand much more about yourself. Also, if you notice your common reactions or weaknesses around triggering people, you can begin to piece together pain points in your own heart. Then, begin to heal these parts of yourself.

Projection

Much like transference only in reverse, projection is when we place our own discomfort onto another. We often hold the burdens of those around us without realizing it. You've heard the phrase, "it's not you, it's me." Well, sometimes it really is the other person. Again, all we can control is ourselves in this picture though. First, we can become aware of when we are projecting our insecurities onto another. Second, we can become aware of when others are projecting their own insecurities onto us.

Whenever you are the victim of judgment, chances are that person is judging you based on their own issues, and it likely has nothing to do with you (and vice versa). I'm sure you can imagine a time when you judged or shamed someone (even if only privately to yourself), but think, did it actually have anything to do with them? Or, perhaps, were you judging someone else based on your own insecurities?

This is a challenging concept with more nuance than the scope of this book allows. My hope for you is that you begin to see beyond the surface, to look beyond the superficial, and to truly see the heart of the matter. Therein lies the truth.

Remember my example about the dishes in Chapter 9? To refresh your memory, I had come home from a stressful 30-hour call shift. The house was a mess and I picked a fight with my husband over the dishes. I bring up this example again, because from all of my patients and clients, I know that the topic of household chores is particularly stressful. What I didn't mention earlier was that I not only fixated on the dishes, but I verbally attacked my husband. I was angry, tired, and frustrated. I had associated cleaning and doing the dishes with love. Therefore, when my husband did not clean or do the dishes, I felt completely unloved. I thus projected my own feelings of unworthiness onto my husband. Essentially, I wanted him to feel as unloved as I felt in that moment.

Pursuer and Withdrawer

In a conflicted relationship, there is always a Pursuer and a Withdrawer. This is not about courtship roles or about authority, obedience, or submission, and it's not a gender thing. These are truly personality characteristics.

The Pursuer is often the more expressive one. While he or she is usually more outgoing and extroverted in nature, this is not always true. Naturally, though, they want to fix problems. When they feel tension or conflict, they want to work through the issues head-on.

The Withdrawer, as the name suggests, naturally retreats. They prefer more introspection and thought analysis before problem-solving occurs. Again, this tends to be more of an introvert by nature. Though, this is unique to how someone responds in a given relationship.

For every relationship, we can either be a Pursuer or a Withdrawer in times of conflict. We can switch between these roles at any given time as well. For instance, I may be more of a Pursuer in conflicts with my husband but more of a Withdrawer in conflicts with my colleagues.

The ideal relationship reigns in these extremes and finds a healthy balance in the middle. When an individual begins spending all of her time as the Pursuer in a given relationship, then the relationship is likely strained. Furthermore, when you are a Withdrawer in every single one of your relationships, then there is likely a deeper issue to be uncovered.

Next time you have an argument or find yourself frustrated with someone, acknowledge which role you are playing. Do you notice a pattern? Becoming aware of your role at any given time within a given relationship can help you know yourself better. Also, it will help you to stop the blanket judgments that arise when a given individual may be triggering you.

Setting Boundaries

It was a typical Sunday morning, one that I happened to be on call at the hospital. I was covering half of the inpatient psychiatric unit with one other psychiatrist on call. It had been a crowded weekend with several new admissions and a skeleton staff. I was sleep deprived from numerous phone calls the night before.

I strolled into the hospital that morning eager to make the rounds with my patients and get my work done as efficiently as possible. I quickly noticed that the unit was hot, meaning there were multiple agitated, aggressive patients on the unit: a few withdrawing from drugs, some acutely psychotic, and others stirring up fights with other patients. Despite popular belief, this is not common for a psychiatric unit. Nonetheless, it's not the first time I've been around an active unit. I assumed that because I would only be there for a few hours, I better just lay low, get my work done, and get out as soon as possible. That was until I interviewed Ms. B.

Ms. B had already been yelling at several staff members that morning. She had pulled down her shirt and revealed her breasts to other patients and was now demanding who-knows-what from the selfless janitor. She begrudgingly agreed to speak with me in the closed interview room. A few moments into our meeting, I heard screaming outside of the door. It was coming from the day treatment room. I heard footsteps running and the sounds of staff breaking up a fight. At the same time, Ms. B was quickly escalating in front of me. In an effort to preserve my personal safety, I slowly directed Ms. B out of the room. Ms. B begrudgingly retreated to her room. I then peered out of the interview room. Before I could assess the situation...

WAM! I was dazed, pain began tingling from the side of my jaw. In the midst of escorting my own agitated patient, the conflict that was brewing outside the exam room collided with me. Literally. I looked around me in an effort to make sense of what just happened. I saw another patient jeering back at me. *Wow,* I thought, *she just popped me in the jaw.* And she wasn't even my patient. Ms. B was thankfully waiting patiently in her room.

Although people warn you that psychiatrists are at higher risk of being physically assaulted by patients, I never thought that it would happen to me. I considered myself to have good instincts around patients. I treated countless severely mentally ill patients throughout residency and never once was hit. While I thankfully did not sustain any lasting injuries, I was taken aback. When someone violates your boundaries, it easily throws you in a funk. Unlike physical boundaries, we cannot see someone's emotional boundaries. You may not even have emotional boundaries at this point.

Hopefully, as you continue this journey, you begin to notice particular stressors, limitations, weaknesses, or mental blocks. As your heart heals, you need a boundary of protection surrounding it. While your mental attitude defenses are the walls around your heart, your new boundaries are like scaffolding around your heart. You may need to create space between you and a friend who is particularly triggering to you. You may need to speak up to your husband who condescends to you. You may need to assert yourself with your boss who critiques you. In the early stages, your heart can be vulnerable. Creating boundaries will serve you well as you continue this journey.

Setbacks and Rejection

Even in the most loving of relationships, we will be let down, and we will let down others. We are all human beings. As such, we are marvelously flawed and imperfect. No matter how grounded or introspective you are, you will inadvertently say the wrong thing, or someone else will hurt your heart. You will face many setbacks and rejections.

Rejection is painful. There are no quips about it. To put your heart on the line is anxiety-provoking enough. Then, to have your heart pummeled to the ground and thrown back at you is nothing short of torture. The most common issue I see when handling rejection, though, is to displace the rejection of us onto something else.

One of the most common displacements of emotional pain is onto our physical bodies. When I was growing up, I wanted to believe that my failed dating relationships were because of my body. I internalized emotional pain to be a purely physical matter. In my flawed understanding, if a boy didn't like me, then it must be because he's not attracted to me physically. If that's the case, then I can just change my body and win him over. I like winning people over. I like winning, period. To lose a relationship brought up many insecurities.

While we don't necessarily have much control over our physical appearance, it seems to be an easy catch-all for our problems. Ironically, we dream of a man loving us for us, yet we hinder that possibility every time we try to conform to the ridiculous beauty standards of our day. Moreover, it becomes difficult to admit to ourselves that someone has rejected us. It's somehow easier to accept that he rejected our body than to accept that he rejected our self. To be rejected personally is painful.

The most important step to take is to allow yourself to feel the pain. Stop placing judgment on yourself in the process. It's the avoidance of pain that often leads to worse, more self-destructive coping. We only utilize said coping skills as a way to suppress emotional pain. The more we can actually feel our feelings, the better we are equipped to ride the wave. After we embrace our emotions, we can then better communicate our needs and handle the next setback that comes our way.

Find Your *HEART*

- 💜 **Here and Now.** Describe a recent conflict or stressful situation with a loved one.
- 💜 **Embrace Your Emotions.** What feelings or emotions arise as you relive this situation?
- 💜 **Analyze Your Thoughts.** How can you interpret the thoughts and feelings in this situation?
- 💜 **Reflect On Your Past.** Have you reacted to a loved one similarly in the past? Did you witness a similar exchange between your own parents?
- 💜 **Take Action.** Set boundaries in your relationship. Have one conversation with a loved one where you share your needs clearly and honestly.

21
Reconnecting with Your Passions

I grew up in a very close-knit family. My brothers were my best friends and my parents were involved in my life. We had many deep conversations. I always felt safe sharing anything and everything that was on my mind. It was not uncommon to wake up and have a Meaning of Life conversation over breakfast. However, there is one part of me that always felt left out, the piece of me that made me feel alien in my family, that one thing that no one else really understood, like a secret I kept hidden from the world. For me, that was music.

As a very young girl, I begged my parents for a year to take piano lessons. I'm sure they wanted to make sure I was going to take it seriously before they allowed me to have lessons, so for a year I begged and pleaded. Finally, they caved and let me take lessons. I never had to be told to practice. I loved playing. The same was true for the violin. I practiced incessantly. I loved the calmness that overtook me when I could create music. I fell in love with orchestra. In junior high, I began singing. My love for musical theater exploded in high school. It was the highlight of my day.

I was extremely gifted as well. I won countless awards in piano, orchestra, and choir. I was selected for elite show choir clubs and was cast in musicals. I even gave a nod to a possible career on Broadway at one point in time. I continued singing some in college and took up songwriting as a hobby. Slowly, though, as my more serious goals of medical school and the desire for a proper social life took precedent, my music-making days dwindled.

To reach excellence in any one area of your life requires the forsaking of almost all others. In pursuit of becoming a doctor, I laid most of my minor hobbies to rest. Somewhere along the line, I allowed external influences to steal this joy from me as well. In an effort to rise up my forgotten passions, I remember one particular conversation with my dad.

"Are you happy?" my dad asked. It seemed to be an odd question, seeing as I had just returned from the emergency department after a serious bout with a stomach bug when I was 11 weeks pregnant with my son, Ryker; likely from the dehydration of diarrhea and vomiting, I had fainted.

We had been visiting my parents for Christmas. I lay on the couch in my childhood home while sucking on a popsicle, hoping I would keep it down and praying that I could tolerate solid foods by Christmas Day. In my current state, talking about my level of happiness seemed bizarre. My dad can be rather deep and random at times, so I went with it.

"Well, yes," I said with reservation.

"Okay, I just want you to know how proud I am of you. All I want is for you to be happy." He grinned. I felt as though he was probing me for more. My parents always had a way of opening me up without ever asking me anything.

"Honestly…" I paused. "I feel like I'm losing myself," I lamented to my dad. Tears began to well up in my eyes. *Darn pregnancy hormones.* "Like here I am… a doctor… doing what I've always dreamed of doing, and I just can't help but think something is missing. I feel like I've given up so much to accomplish this one goal, and I've given up so many other parts of myself," I rambled on. "I miss my hobbies and social life and friends."

My dad just listened.

"You know, sometimes I think of my grandmothers," I paused. I don't know if I had ever told him that before. My mom's mom and my dad's mom both died before I was born. Both of my parents say that I remind them of their mothers. I'm built like my dad's mom, I share personality traits with my mom's mom, and I get my musical talents from both of them.

He became quiet. "Well, they would've loved you."

"I think I would've enjoyed making music with them," I said quietly to myself. "I really miss music, dad," I admitted. It hit me like a ton of bricks. I don't know why it wasn't clear before.

Music had been the through-story of my life. It weaved together all the parts of my soul. I would not only consume music, but I would produce music. Music helped me cope with a lifelong rollercoaster of emotions, from joy to sadness and anger to grief. Music was not only a hobby but a passion. When I would go into exam days in college, I used to tell myself, *Well, if I fail this test, at least I have music.* Music was one of the things that brought me and my husband together. Travis and I have joked about having a family band one day. We still dream of having a grand piano and concert hall in our big mansion one day.

At the time of the tearful conversation with my dad, music was a distant past. My piano skills were shabby, my violin was out of tune, and my vocal cords were rusty. I no longer wrote songs, mashed playlists, or jammed out with friends. I even traded in my karaoke car rides for audiobooks, church sermons, and personal development podcasts. Since then, I have slowly incorporated music back into my life. While I may never be lead singer in a rock band or have a starring role in the next hit Broadway musical, I can sing out my girl power anthems and record song lyrics in my journal. And I can finally learn to play the guitar.

Reconnecting with a lost love feels like coming home. It's as if a part of yourself was missing and now you are more complete. We're pretty brilliant as kids. We know what we like and what we don't like. We are not hindered by the judgment of society or opinions of others. Hopefully, we had a grown-up or two who encouraged us to pursue those activities that brought us pure joy. In that essence, we can learn a lot about ourselves by reflecting on our younger selves and rekindling those beloved passions.

This is also the time I tell you that not all of our passions stem from childhood, and not all of our passions end in excellence. Growing up, I hated running. Rather, I didn't see the point in it. I always viewed it as a punishment or a means to an end. I never viewed running as an enjoyable hobby in and of itself. Not to mention I was very slow. In my eighth-grade cross country team, I came in next-to-last place in the only meet that I even qualified to compete in.

The next time I took running seriously was when I took a running class in college. Again, I was one of the slowest people in my class. My instructor was a former collegiate cross-country runner who had the personality of a chipper cheerleader. Despite her overwhelming enthusiasm, I never quite developed the itch for running. When the class concluded, I stopped running.

Three years later, I started medical school. The beginning of medical school is like drinking from a fire hose: so much information, so little time, so much stress. Where you once were the big fish in a little pond, now you're the guppy in the ocean. You're surrounded by equally brilliant and accomplished individuals, all vying for the same thing. While my medical school class was more collegial and supportive than others, it's the internal drive to succeed that wears you down. The mounting pressure before my first round of exams was intense.

One day, I pulled on my workout clothes, laced up my tennis shoes, put on my headphones, blasted my pump-up jams, and started running. For the first time since beginning medical school, I felt free. I could escape. Running relieved my stress in the rough years of medical school. I came to love running for how it made me feel. I followed the lead of some of my classmates and began training for my first half-marathon. After that, I was hooked. I then trained for my first marathon. Training for a marathon is such symbolism for our daily grind and particularly fitting for that time in my life. Little did I know that I was building up endurance to withstand several more years of trials and pressures of medical training.

I went on to run seven more marathons and one more half-marathon. I really loved running. I even had pipedreams of doing an ultramarathon or training for an Olympic marathon. Despite all of the running I have done, I have never been a fast runner. To this day, I am not a good runner. Popular opinion would say that you should spend your time doing what you're good at. From a young age, my father told me that "your best is the best." There may have been some truth to his words, as I was able to reach a level of excellence in many things that I ventured. However, I also developed a belief that if I was not the best, then I was failing. And if I was not the best, then it wasn't worth my time.

These comments from well-intentioned adults can dramatically affect us. We intertwine our passions with only the activities and hobbies that we can excel at. While skill in a craft can indeed bolster confidence, especially in young children, we do not need to remove activities that we love doing simply because we are not the best at them.

If you love cooking but you are not that great, please do not stop cooking. If you love crafts but you have never mastered a Pinterest-worthy project, please do not stop crafting. (Also know you're a girl after my own heart.) If you love dancing but you can't keep a beat, please do not stop dancing. You need not be great at something to benefit from the powerful state of flow that comes from doing something that you love doing, and you may indeed improve as you continue practicing the craft.

You cannot control what you love. You *can* control how you spend your time. You will likely bring more abundance and joy to your life when you do things you love to do rather than things you are just good at doing. When you are good at everything you do, life is no longer a challenge. Boredom then creeps in. Adding a challenging task or a fulfilling hobby builds up the complexity of life, leading to more fulfillment and engagement. Plus, being bad at something is extremely humbling. I may never run a marathon in under four hours, but it won't stop me from enjoying the sport of running. Owning our joys, even when they result in failures, is the name of the game.

Making time for activities that bring us joy will help us live from the heart. The desires of your heart are not by coincidence. There is a divine purpose and plan for you. Pursuing your interests is one critical move that will help you unapologetically be you.

Find Your *HEART*

- ♥ **Here and Now.** How much time do you spend doing activities for pure joy?
- ♥ **Embrace Your Emotions.** How does it feel to acknowledge lost hobbies or passions?
- ♥ **Analyze Your Thoughts.** Why do you feel that you can't engage in actions or behaviors that bring you joy?
- ♥ **Reflect On Your Past.** What made you stop these pursuits in your past? How did it feel to engage in these hobbies in your glory days?
- ♥ **Take Action.** Take up a childhood hobby. You may or may not still have skill in this area of your life. Don't let that hold you back. Even if you are not great at it, failure can be freeing and humbling in its own right.

22
Find Your Tribe

"Stefani…" Maddy said softly through the door. "Knock, knock. Is anyone home in here?" She gently peered through the slightly cracked door.

"Yes, I'm here," I groaned. I barely looked up at her from my desk. I was sitting in front of my computer staring at my Excel spreadsheet with tentative wedding plans and timelines.

"Are you… um… okay? You've been a little… hermit-y the last few weeks." She was right. Since Travis went back on deployment, I had retreated. I hadn't gone out with my friends. I'd barely made it to class, which I didn't have to go to thanks to video recorded lectures. I wasn't eating much. I had watched way too many YouTube videos that showed soldiers coming home to their families and girlfriends. I was grieving. My life had been diminished to class work and Skype dates with Travis.

"Yeah, I'm okay." It was a gut response. Why do we feel as though we are not allowed to be "not okay?" The love of my life and best friend and now fiancé had just recently returned to Iraq for the last eight months of his deployment. Clearly, I was not okay.

"Okkkkaaayyyy…" Maddy repeated. She called my bluff. "Well, why don't we get out and go to dinner tonight? We can go get Michelle. I'll ask some other people what they're up to."

"Yeah, I could eat, I guess," I said flatly.

"Come on, it'll be good for you." It's amazing when friends truly know you better than you know yourself.

That night out was freedom. For the first time in several weeks, I could take my mind off of Travis and reconnect with my moment-to-moment life. As I laughed over dinner and drinks with good friends at our favorite local restaurant, I felt warmth in my heart. I never had many girlfriends growing up. Having two brothers made it easier for me to fit in with the guys than the girls. My mom used to remark that girls were probably intimidated by me. Truth be told, I was probably intimidated by them. Out of my own insecurity, I stuck to my comfort zone and didn't have many friends.

When I joined a sorority in college, I formed lasting girl friendships for the first time in my life. The more I showed my true colors, the more I received genuine connections in return. I have countless examples of these "super sweet sisterhood moments," as my college sorority called it. I can't even begin to name all of my favorite memories with dear friends. Some friendships have been in my life for a reason or a season, and a select few will be there to the grave.

We all want the forever friends. We dream of the movie-inspired friendships where we finish each other's sentences and know everything about each other. While I do have a few friends like this, it is the exception, not the rule. It took me a long time to find and keep friends like this. As with any lasting relationship, we must be ready to receive that blessing. My immaturity and fears held me back from bonding with many girls for many years. I had the limiting belief that girls were "jealous" of me, a line fed to me by some well-meaning adults. Maybe they were right, but maybe it was I that was jealous of them. I projected my own insecurities onto them.

This is a fairly common occurrence among women. A long-term patient of mine, Rae, had a challenging time with her friendships.

"What's on your mind?" I asked opening up our weekly therapy session.

"Oh, I'm really anxious today for some reason. You know my friend Caitlin? Well, I just always feel like she is purposefully leaving me out or something." She appeared noticeably anxious today, sitting up straight, shaking her foot, fiddling her hands in her hair.

"And?" Sometimes all it takes is one word to lead a person to their own solutions. My supervisor in residency called this "the mental tap."

"And… it's frustrating. I feel left out. Like yesterday, I kept texting her to see if she wanted me to come over and bring her food. I had been asking all week. She never got back to me. I know she would've liked it since she was home with the baby and all. Well, she never even texted me back."

"Okay?" I tapped.

"But then I found out today that she had our other friend Jackie visit her yesterday. They must've planned this already and she never even said anything to me." Rae went to high school with Caitlin and Jackie. From what I could gather, they were all still close friends. They were an acting part of each other's lives. As with all friendships, they may have just needed space.

"That sounds frustrating," I reflected back.

"Yes, yes it is." She smiled in anger before she continued, "It didn't used to be this way you know? I mean, I remember it being different," she lamented. After each having a child in the last year, their relationships had likely changed. I see this dynamic shift in many new moms. It's an act of grieving the life that you once had and learning to enjoy the beauty of the present day.

"Of course, it was different. You each didn't have babies or husbands in tow," I said sincerely. I fully know the pain she feels of wanting to connect with moms but feeling torn between your former self and your current self. *Who am I anyway?*

"Yeah… I just wish it was easier," Rae said annoyingly. She slouched in her chair, appearing exhausted over what seemed to be a lengthy analysis.

"Wish what was easier?" I inquired.

"I don't know… being friends. Having friends. Social life with friends." She rambled.

"Like what would you imagine?" I could already make my own hypothesis here. Rae had moved back to her hometown after years away at college and graduate school. Most of her childhood friends also lived in her hometown. She was now married to her high school sweetheart, and they had a new three-month-old baby.

"I guess… it's just…" she paused. She looked up, as if she was thoroughly planning out her next choice of words. "Like I wish we all lived close to each other and we could just walk to each other's houses and stuff."

"Like… when you were kids?" I interpreted.

"Haha, yeah I guess so," she laughed nervously. Usually when I make interpretations like this out loud, it stops my patients in their tracks. It's important to state the obvious sometimes.

"And is that realistic?" I smiled.

"I guess not." She looked down. I saw the whirling of sadness and realization wash over her face.

Setting realistic expectations is important for all walks of life, but especially important in friendships. In our world influenced by *Friends* and social media, we can easily develop an extremely skewed version of reality. We either idealize virtual friendships or acquaintances, or we burden genuine friendships with wanna-be-TV-inspired-dramatized relationships, neither of which are realistic.

Apart from having a skewed vision of what friendship should look like, we also weakly assume that friendships should always be a stable entity of our lives. For one, no matter how close our friends are, they are not a permanent fixture in our lives. Also, just as our sense of self will mold and morph over time, our friendships will adapt as well. In order to maintain old friendships or build new relationships, we must be willing to consent to the ever-evolving change in role. While we need to be ourselves to make friendships in the first place, we also have to be flexible enough to adapt to new circumstances.

When we can be adaptable, we also receive the blessing of connecting with amazingly different individuals who can touch and inspire us in ways we never dreamed possible. We also stop ignoring our hearts and allow flexibility even in the most unique of friendships. For me, I've always had a knack for finding the most unique friends. Since I was a little girl, I've had an eclectic array of friends. It wasn't ever something I consciously worked on, but I truly enjoyed being around people who seemed most authentic to me. It's so refreshing to be around people who are… real. As you know, those people can be a part of several different circles. I had preppy friends and jock friends, goth friends and music friends, "in crowd" friends and "outsider" friends. I never quite fit into any mold.

It's funny talking to high school or college friends now. They usually are shocked to find out details of my other personas. My academic friends didn't know about my social life. My social friends didn't know about my career goals and aspirations. My church friends didn't know about my interests and hobbies. My music and golf friends didn't know my family or social friends. This fragmentation is even more common as a mother and a wife. Few fellow military wives know much about my interests, unique characteristics, or who I am as a person. Other preschool parents barely know my husband's name or where I'm from. Work colleagues don't know my beliefs or what's important to me. And most people don't know what I do for a living.

I'm not suggesting that you now go out and tell all of your friends every detail about yourself. There can be valid reasons why we choose not to disclose certain parts of ourselves with different people in our lives. We can uphold our right to privacy in any way we choose. I am suggesting that, in the fragmentation of self, we have veiled ourselves. Instead of wearing different hats, we started to wear different masks, completely cloaking our identity. In an effort to be all things to all people, we have forgotten who we are. We have become afraid of showing our true selves. Friendships and community are bountiful blessings in this world. When our internal sense of self suffers from any given friendship or community, it is time to reflect. I've been truly blessed to have a select few friends who love me, friends who are more like sisters, who have seen me through thick and thin, who truly get me. (To you amazing people in my life, you know who you are. I love you. You have made my life richer and fuller. You are a blessing.) Guess what? Friends like you because you are you. Ironically, when I stopped trying to fit in and started living my life more authentically, my friendships began blossoming as well.

Unfortunately, when I became a mother, my friendships adapted as well. Finding and kindling friendships as a mom can be challenging. After I had Kate, I sought community in all the traditional ways—in-person, online, meet-ups, church groups—but I never seemed to fit in anywhere. I was a working mother, and not only did most working women I knew NOT have children, but I also didn't click with all of them anyway. And because I was a working mom, I couldn't relate to stay at home moms. I was younger than other doctor moms. I was a breastfeeding mom, but I wasn't that hardcore. I was a red-wine-on-Fridays kind of mom, but I was such a homebody. I never got out much. I was a fit mom, but I was also realistic with my limits. I was a fashionable mom, but I was still in my maternity pants. I was a military mom, but I didn't know any other military moms near me at the time. I was also totally overwhelmed by all the options for mom communities. If you didn't know, there's about a bazillion "mom communities" out there.

There are the fit moms, the sporty moms, the crunchy moms, the healthy moms, the boss moms, the working moms, the stay at home moms, the work at home moms, the volunteer moms, the tech moms, the blogger moms, the book club moms, the religious moms, the zen moms, the MILF moms, the doctor moms, the military moms, the fashionista moms, the sexy moms, the corporate moms, the artsy moms, the foodie moms, the party moms, the baby-wearing moms, the breastfeed-at-all-costs moms, the bad moms, the scary moms, and everything in between… I was all of these things and none of these things at the same time. I just didn't quite fit any one "type." I drove myself crazy trying to be everything to everyone. I felt guilty for being a working mom, not because I didn't love my job—I love what I do—but because of some external standard that working moms can't be good moms. I also thought I was wrong for starting an online business… I mean, who am I? I'm still working full time, raising kids and starting a business. I let my inner naysayer get me down a lot. I often downplayed who I was for fear that some other mom would judge me. I know I'm not alone in this.

Here's the thing, none of us really fit the stereotypes set forth by us. Why don't we stop pretending like we do? Why do we feel like we have to keep following these self-inflicting rules and standards? And why don't we just be the kind of mom we want to be with fierce confidence?

Then, in an act of divine download, it struck me. I don't fit the typical mom groups, because I am not the typical mom. In that moment, Not the Typical Mom™ community was born: a community to encourage moms to escape the stereotypes and abolish the mom guilt. Not the Typical Mom™ was a platform to help moms embrace their real selves and find their own way, without judgment or guilt. While I no longer run the community, I still love connecting with fellow not-so-typical moms. Be sure to connect with me on social media and share your own unique motherhood story.

23
CONCLUSION
From the Bottom of My Heart

I remember the day like it was yesterday. I was crumpled on the floor of the shower. The hot water had turned cold. Travis was out running errands. Baby Kate was sleeping soundly. I only heard the sounds of running water and my golden retriever Trooper's deep breathing. He was lying on the cold floor outside the shower waiting for me to emerge from the steam-filled bathroom. *Dogs really do have a sixth sense*, I thought. It was Trooper that noticed when I was first pregnant, and he always becomes a little more clingy and attentive when I'm under more stress.

Shwoooooooshh... the sound of the cold water beating down on me. I wished it was loud enough to drown out my thoughts.

How could you be feeling like this?

You're a new mom.

A new doctor.

Living in a beautiful home.

You have a life that so many would die for.

My thoughts attacked me. Restless and formulaic.

I wrestled with myself. *Dear Lord, take this burden from*

me. I can't do it. I've hit my max. Carry me through this. I'm weak without you. You are my only strength. So many prayers.

I know now that He answered them all, in His way and in His time, but that moment in the shower... My stomach turns weak just thinking about it. The razor blades. All I remember are the razor blades, my razor sitting next to Travis's, like two peas in a pod. All I ever wanted was a man I could share a home with, make a family with, build a life with. And now, who am I? I don't feel like myself. I imagine how I could use the razor blades. I don't really want to end my life. I do think about death though. What if I just went to sleep and didn't wake up?

Then, in my dream like state, I hear the words... *You've got heart.*

And an impetus inside of me pushes me forward.

I need to get out of the shower. *Get out of the shower,* I commanded myself.

Stand up.

Rinse shampoo out of hair.

No time for conditioner. The baby is crying now. I continue the commands.

Turn off water.

Grab towel.

Step out of shower.

Dry off.

So methodical. So formulaic. *That's what this is,* I tell myself. An experiment. Is it real? *Yes, this is real.* I am a mother. *This is my baby. This is my life.* I look at the clock. 1:28... when will Travis get back? *He just went to the store,* I assure myself.

I don't remember the exact date. It must have been December. I think I was on my Emergency Medicine rotation. Shift work. Just as my circadian rhythms were coming back into alignment postpartum, I throw in the ever-changing nights-to-days, days-to-nights pattern for emergency department shifts into the mix. I worked through the holidays. It didn't feel like December. I worked on Christmas Day. I was halfway across the

236

country from my family and closest friends. I barely remember shopping for Christmas presents. I managed to put up a Christmas tree and some household decorations. I was always able to put on a good face.

It's funny that people depict depressed people as these haggard, unkempt souls bound to the confines of their bed without food or awareness of reality. I was none of those things. Maybe it's the Texas girl in me, but from the outside, I never went a day without makeup. I smiled and laughed with my patients and colleagues at work. I cooked. I cleaned. I cared for my daughter. I walked my dog. I went to work. I even kept it spicy in the bedroom with my husband (well, tried to).

To the outside world, I probably looked like a beautifully-wrapped Christmas present. My friend calls this "glossy depression," and I, my friends, was definitely "glossy." Little did people know, I was empty. I was drowning inside. I felt as though I was drowning and just barely treading water most days. You know how hard it is to tread water? That's how I felt. Every. Single. Day. For nine months.

Kay Redfield Jamison, clinical psychologist and bestselling author of *An Unquiet Mind*, detailing her experience with bipolar disorder, describes the difference between depression and a bad day. Out of a bad day comes creativity, but nothing comes out of depression. It's true. My depression stole all of the creativity of my soul. Little by little, my soul was suffocating into a black hole. I couldn't really see it happening until I was too far in, and by then, I couldn't stop it. I had to escape. I had to find a way out.

I will never know how I got myself up off that shower floor. To this day, I feel as though my guardian angel actually lifted me up. But what came next was a true Godsend. I first became aware of my pain in the here and now. I told my husband about some of my dark thoughts and told him I thought I needed help. I assumed he would judge me or convince me I just needed to pray more. Instead, he said, "I agree, Stefani. I think you need help. We'll get you help."

Ahhh... just like that, my road to recovery began. I breathed a sigh of relief and in that moment, it was as though a million pounds of bricks were lifted from my shoulders. I felt a peace and lightness that I didn't know I could feel. Just giving myself permission to get help was transcendent above all my current struggles.

Whether you face the darkness of clinical depression or the burn-out of daily living, losing your heart is never a welcome affair. It is slow and subtle. It creeps through the floorboard of your conscience until you wake up and no longer recognize yourself. Then, one day, you wake up to reality. You realize that this isn't all there is, that God has restored your heart for more than this.

After I overcame postpartum depression, I began picking up the pieces of my heart and mending the scars of my soul. I started embracing my emotions. Sometimes they were painful. Other times they were heartwarming. I began feeling better physically and mentally. I began feeling myself. I began leading a life from within, rather than conforming to the standards of ambiguous, earthly limitations.

Until then, I felt like I could never be my real self. I had plagued the real me with shame, blame, and guilt. I wasn't passive enough, pretty enough, thin enough, quiet enough, liberal enough, or conservative enough. I wasn't the best wife or mother or daughter or sister or doctor. And I had a raging current of pain that I was afraid to feel. I believed at an unconscious level that my pain was not worthy, that I was a bad Christian and a bad mom for experiencing depression.

The climb out of the darkness was not easy. The journey back to my heart was not smooth. I analyzed and questioned all aspects of my life. I asked myself why I was doing what I was doing, and how I came to be who I was. Five years were spent breaking the rules, setting my own standards, assessing my relationships, changing my thoughts, feeling my feelings, processing my past, and refining my heart. I reflected on my pain points. I read and researched anything and everything I could find. Then, I tossed it all to the curb, knowing that all I ever needed to know was right inside of me. I began listening to my heart, feeling my heartbeat. The process is slow and subtle. Some days are good. Some days are bad. One day, you'll take two steps forward. The next, you'll take ten steps backward.

Only now can I truly say this: I have finally accepted myself. I have reconnected with all the parts of me, good and bad. I embrace my heart, the most essential part of me. I look back on my younger self with so much awe, and I begin to realize that I am still her and she is still me. Her heart beats deep inside me. While I may not be an Olympic gymnast, I am the same outspoken, stubborn fireball. I may have tempered the blaze of fire here and there, but I'll never lose my glow. And the glow shines from deep within my heart.

I have redefined my heart. My heart is not a thread of accomplishments, a conglomeration of things, or a collection of people. My heart is not even a compilation of heartaches, failures, and painful memories. My heart is the ever-beating essence of me.

Our greatest essence will ebb and flow with the tides. We will transform and adapt throughout life. It is the continual renewal of our minds and the never-ending journey to our hearts that make this life worth living, and our purposes worth pursuing. What I now see is this: the greatest part of us is the part we most fear to show to the world. It is also the only part that can live out our divine purpose on this planet.

Now, instead of dreaming of the glory and riches of this world, I dream of my legacy for eternity. I dream of fulfilling my purpose on this earth to fulfill God's purposes hereafter. I have a dream that our daughters will one day live in a world where they are judged not by the details of their lives, but by the depth of their hearts. When I imagine a world of women living from their hearts, I feel full inside. I see an environment of encouragement and accomplished dreams, where women stop fretting the details of life and start living their freaking lives.

I'm not talking about utopia. We do live in the Devil's world, remember? I am talking about truly embracing the desires of your heart without the guilt and shame. I am talking about living your life the way you want to live your life, without the incessant judgment. I am talking about accomplishing the goals that bring you lasting joy, not a conditional hope of joy from some flawed premise. I am talking about freeing yourself from the burdens of your heart that are holding you back and keeping you small.

This is not a political problem. This is not a social problem. This is a *you* problem. This is a problem of the heart. No outside influence will ever change your heart. Your heart is inside of you. It's inside all of us. Awaken your soul. Feel your feelings. Live from within. Embrace your spirit. More than anything...

Let your heart out.

Work With Me

Thank you for reading this book! I hope I've encouraged you to let your heart out. I'd really love to connect with you further! There are many ways to connect.

Start Here

To learn more about the HEART Method and hear all about my latest online offerings, be sure to visit my main site at www.letyourheartout.com.

It's Not About the Food

For specific guidance and encouragement about food and body image struggles, you'll enjoy my *It's Not About the Food* online course. Sign up for my free video series at www.notaboutthefood.com.

Attack Anxiety Masterclass

If you are struggling to change your thought distortions, sign up for my free trainings at www.attackanxietynow.com.

Blog

To keep in touch and hear about all of my latest online offerings, go to my main site at www.notthetypicalmom.com.

Individuals

If you are a resident of Texas or Virginia and interested in individual mental health services or professional supervision, please visit www.stefanireinoldmd.com for more information.

Professionals

I love connecting with fellow mental health or perinatal professionals. I offer supervision, mentorship, and guidance for women's mental health issues and eating disorders. Please reach out to me at www.stefanireinoldmd.com for more information.

Acknowledgements

I have to first thank my Lord and Savior, Jesus Christ. Without you, I am nothing. I thank you Lord for granting me so many talents and spiritual gifts. May I continue to be an instrument for your grace and love.

I thank my amazing, supportive, and loving husband, Travis. Thank you for helping care for the children while I wrote this book. And for believing in me all those years ago that I would one day be an author. Thank you for all the bath times and play dates that you handled in my absence of writing this book. And thank you for allowing me to be transparent in our own stories from the heart. Baby, you are my best friend. You have helped me see my heart more than anyone else. I'm forever grateful for your loyalty, dedication, and love for me. You are my one and only.

Thank you to my wonderful children, Kate and Ryker. Being a mother is the most paramount role I will ever play in my life. Kate, you are the most beautiful, funny, articulate, and spunky daughter. You bring joy to my days. Ryker, you are the sweetest, most sensitive boy. I'm truly enjoying watching you grow up. You two bring light to my life. I love seeing the world through your playful eyes and simple means. You give me the platform to share my heart each and every day.

243

To my mom, thank you. Thank you for all of your sacrifices—financially, emotionally, physically. You placed me, Kristofer, and Gavin before your own needs always. I can only dream of being the selfless mother that you were to me. You helped mature my emotional side and see the deeper current of life. You helped me see my heart. I love you so much.

Thank you, dad. You were the driving force for so many of my accomplishments. Always thinking outside of the box, you taught me to see the world through a different lens. You encouraged me to be me and never give up on my dreams. Your wisdom, creativity, and charisma continue to light up a room. I love you.

To my amazing brothers, Kristofer and Gavin. I'd never be who, what, or where I am today without you two. You have been my rocks when I needed stability. You have been my clowns when I needed humor. You both have made me feel like a precious jewel. Through thick and through thin, you are always there when I need you most. You allow me to be the cream in the Oreo cookie. No brothers are as great as y'all. Love you both.

Thank you to Morgan and my amazing team at Paper Raven Books. Morgan, you were my biggest cheerleader, always encouraging and making this book debut the best experience possible. Victoria, my production manager, thank you. This book would not be possible without your leadership and guidance. Sarah, my developmental editor, you truly helped me capture my message, and I thank you for helping me find clarity. Darcy, thank you for your encouragement and guidance in making this book the best possible. Michael, thank you for your attention to detail and expertise. Jesus, you truly worked magic with my book and I thank you. Amanda and Rachela, you helped make my launch seamless and stress-free. Karen, thank you for being the glue in the team, helping us all (and me in particular) stay organized and focused.

Thank you to Shalon and Dana from The Ironroad Group for creating such a beautiful foundational brand for me. Thank

244

you to Amanda and Susannah of Authentic Portrait for my beautiful brand photography. Little did I know when I hired photographers that I would be meeting new friends.

Thank you to my friends, family, patients, and clients whom I cite in this book. Your stories have been interwoven in mine and I am so grateful that your hearts have become a part of mine.

Last but not least, thank you readers! Without you, my book is just words on a page. You make me a real author. I hope you enjoyed my debut book. I look forward to your readership with many more books in the future.

Works Cited, in chronological order

Chapter 2

1. National Association of Eating Disorders. (n.d.). *National Eating Disorders.* Retrieved November 5, 2017, from www.nationaleatingdisorders.org/index.php

2. Ross, C. (2015). *Why Do Women Hate Their Bodies?* Retrieved Nov 3, 2017, from Psych Central: https://psychcentral.com/blog/archives/2012/06/02/why-do-women-hate-their-bodies/

3. Blond, A. (2008). Impacts of exposure to images of ideal bodies on male body dissatisfaction a review. 5(3), 244-250.

4. Andrea Barrocas, B. H. (2012, Jul). Rates of Nonsuicidal Self-injury in Youth: Age, Sex, and Behavioral Methods in a Community Sample. 130(1), 39-45.

Chapter 3

5. Lindner, M. (2009, January 15). *What People Are Still Willing to Pay For.* Retrieved November 5, 2017, from Forbes: https://www.forbes.com/2009/01/15/self-help-industry-ent-sales-cx_ml_0115selfhelp.html

6. *Why Diets Don't Work: Study Says Dieting Can Actually Cause Weight Gain In the Long Term.* (2012, April 26). (Huffington Post) Retrieved November 7, 2017, from Huffington Post: https://www.huffingtonpost.com/2012/04/25/why-diets-dont-work-long-term-cause-weight-gain_n_1452875.html

7. Lipton, B. (2012, February 7). *Epigenetics.* Retrieved November 7, 2017, from Bruce Lipton: https://www.brucelipton.com/resource/article/epigenetics

8. *It's Now a Proven Fact- Your Unconscious Mind is Running Your Life!* (n.d.). Retrieved November 7, 2017, from Life Trainings: http://www.lifetrainings.com/Your-unconscious-mind-is-running-you-life.html

Chapter 4

9. Rakic, P. (2002, January). Neurogenesis in adult primate neocortex: an evaluation of the evidence. *Nature Reviews Neuroscience, 3*(1), 65-71.

10. Pascual-Leone, A., Freitas, C., Oberman, L., Horvath, J., Halko, M., Eldaief, M., & al., e. (2011). Characterizing brain cortical plasticity and network dynamics across the age-span in health and disease with TMS-EEG and TMS-fMRI. *Brain Topography, 24,* 302-315.

11. Shedler, J. (2010, February-March). The Efficacy of Psychodynamic Psychotherapy. *American Psychologist*, 98-109.

12. Michael Chaiton, L. D. (2016, January). Estimating the number of quit attempts it takes to quit smoking successfully in a longitudinal cohort of smokers. *BMJ Open*, 6(6).

13. National Domestic Violence Hotline. (2013, June 10). 50 Obstacles to Leaving: 1-10. Retrieved November 7, 2017, from e Hotline: http://www.thehotline.org/2013/06/10/50-obstacles-to-leaving-1-10/

14. Anorexia nervosa and related eating disorders. (n.d.). Treatment and Recovery. Retrieved   November 7, 2017, from ANRED: anorexia nervosa and related eating disorders: https://www.anred.com/tx.html

Chapter 5

15. National Institute of Drug Abuse. (n.d.). *National Institute of Drug Abuse.* Retrieved November 5, 2017, from https://www.drugabuse.gov/publications/drugfacts/nationwide-trends

16. Pearlstein, T., Howard, M., Salisbury, A., & Zlotnick, C. (2009, April). Postpartum depression. *200*(4), 357-64.

Chapter 7

17. Brenner, J. D. (2017, November). Neuroimagine in Posttraumatic Stress Disorder and Other Stress-related Disorders. *Neuroimaging Clinical North America, 17*(4), 523-ix.

Bibliography, in alphabetical order

Andrea Barrocas, B. H. (2012, Jul). Rates of Nonsuicidal Self-injury in Youth: Age, Sex, and Behavioral Methods in a Community Sample. 130(1), 39-45.

Anorexia nervosa and related eating disorders. (n.d.). Treatment and Recovery. Retrieved November 7, 2017, from ANRED: anorexia nervosa and related eating disorders: https://www.anred.com/tx.html

Blond, A. (2008). Impacts of exposure to images of ideal bodies on male body dissatisfaction a review. 5(3), 244-250.

Brenner, J. D. (2017, November). Neuroimaging in Posttraumatic Stress Disorder and Other Stress-related Disorders. Neuroimaging Clinical North America, 17(4), 523-ix.

Brian A. Primac, A. S.-V. (2017, April). Use of multiple social media platforms and symptoms of depression and anxiety: A nationally-representative study among U.S. young adults. Computers in Human Behavior, 69, 1-9.

Carolyn Coker Ross, M. (n.d.). Why Do Women Hate Their Bodies? Retrieved November 5, 2017, from Psych Central:

https://psychcentral.com/blog/archives/2012/06/02/why-do-women-hate-their-bodies/

It's Now a Proven Fact- Your Unconscious Mind is Running Your Life! (n.d.). Retrieved November 7, 2017, from Life Trainings: http://www.lifetrainings.com/Your-unconscious-mind-is-running-you-life.html

J., M. P. (2014, January 19). Facebook enhances antidepressant pharmacotherapy effects. Scientific World Journal, ecollection.

JA, N., KA, A., Marsch, L., & Bartels, S. (2016, April). The future of mental health care: peer-to-peer support and social media. Epidemiology of Psychiatric Science, 25(2), 113-122.

Lindner, M. (2009, January 15). What People Are Still Willing to Pay For. Retrieved November 5, 2017, from Forbes: https://www.forbes.com/2009/01/15/self-help-industry-ent-sales-cx_ml_0115selfhelp.html

Lipton, B. (2012, February 7). Epigenetics. Retrieved November 7, 2017, from Bruce Lipton: https://www.brucelipton.com/resource/article/epigenetics

Michael Chaiton, L. D. (2016, January). Estimating the number of quit attempts it takes to quit smoking successfully in a longitudinal cohort of smokers. BMJ Open, 6(6).

National Association of Eating Disorders. (n.d.). National Eating Disorders. Retrieved November 5, 2017, from www.nationaleatingdisorders.org/index.php

National Institute of Drug Abuse. (n.d.). National Institute of Drug Abuse. Retrieved November 5, 2017, from https://www.drugabuse.gov/publications/drugfacts/nationwide-trends

Pascual-Leone, A., Freitas, C., Oberman, L., Horvath, J., Halko, M., Eldaief, M., & al., e. (2011). Characterizing brain cortical plasticity and network dynamics across the age-span in health and disease with TMS-EEG and TMS-fMRI. Brain Topography, 24, 302-315.

Pearlstein, T., Howard, M., Salisbury, A., & Zlotnick, C. (2009, April). Postpartum depression. 200(4), 357-64.

Rakic, P. (2002, January). Neurogenesis in adult primate neocortex: an evaluation of the evidence. Nature Reviews Neuroscience, 3(1), 65-71.

Ross, C. (2015). Why Do Women Hate Their Bodies? Retrieved Nov 3, 2017, from Psych Central: https://psychcentral.com/blog/archives/2012/06/02/why-do-women-hate-their-bodies/

Shedler, J. (2010, February-March). The Efficacy of Psychodynamic Psychotherapy. American Psychologist, 98-109.

The National Domestic Violence Hotline. (2013, June 10). 50 Obstacles to Leaving: 1-10. Retrieved November 7, 2017, from The Hotline: http://www.thehotline.org/2013/06/10/50-obstacles-to-leaving-1-10/

Why Diets Don't Work: Study Says Dieting Can Actually Cause Weight Gain In the Long Term. (2012, April 26). (Huffington Post) Retrieved November 7, 2017, from Huffington Post: https://www.huffingtonpost.com/2012/04/25/why-diets-dont-work-long-term-cause-weight-gain_n_1452875.html

Made in the USA
San Bernardino, CA
15 January 2019